Counterinsurgency in a Test Tube

Analyzing the Success of the Regional Assistance Mission to Solomon Islands (RAMSI)

Russell W. Glenn

Prepared for the
United States Joint Forces Command

NATIONAL DEFENSE
RESEARCH INSTITUTE

The research described in this report was prepared for the United States Joint Forces Command. The research was conducted in the RAND National Defense Research Institute, a federally funded research and development center sponsored by the Office of the Secretary of Defense, the Joint Staff, the Unified Combatant Commands, the Department of the Navy, the Marine Corps, the defense agencies, and the defense Intelligence Community under Contract DASW01-01-C-0004.

Library of Congress Cataloging-in-Publication Data is available for this document.

ISBN: 978-0-8330-4027-5

The RAND Corporation is a nonprofit research organization providing objective analysis and effective solutions that address the challenges facing the public and private sectors around the world. RAND's publications do not necessarily reflect the opinions of its research clients and sponsors.

RAND® is a registered trademark.

Published 2007 by the RAND Corporation
1776 Main Street, P.O. Box 2138, Santa Monica, CA 90407-2138
1200 South Hayes Street, Arlington, VA 22202-5050
4570 Fifth Avenue, Suite 600, Pittsburgh, PA 15213-2665
RAND URL: http://www.rand.org/
To order RAND documents or to obtain additional information, contact
Distribution Services: Telephone: (310) 451-7002;
Fax: (310) 451-6915; Email: order@rand.org

Preface

On July 24, 2003, a joint, multinational, interagency force landed in the Solomon Islands at the request of that nation's prime minister. Its intent was to "reinforce and uphold the legitimate institutions and authorities in the Solomon Islands, and to ensure respect for the country's constitution and implementation of its laws."[1] The call for help came after years of turmoil during which the legitimacy and effectiveness of the Solomon Islands government had been undermined by social strife, corruption, intimidation, and armed groups acting with no regard for the law. Within weeks, the worst of the problems had been suppressed and national rebuilding began. This analysis considers why the Regional Assistance Mission to Solomon Islands (RAMSI) succeeded in its first weeks, months, and years, and what lessons of value its operations might offer to counterinsurgency (COIN) and reconstruction efforts in Afghanistan, Iraq, and elsewhere.

The document will be of interest to individuals in or supporting the government sector whose responsibilities include planning, policy, doctrine, training, or execution of insurgency, counterinsurgency, or other stability operations. It will similarly be of value to students, analysts, or others with a general interest in such undertakings and in the Solomon Islands mission in particular.

This research was sponsored by the Joint Urban Operations Office, J9, Joint Forces Command, and conducted within the International Security and Defense Policy Center of the RAND National

---

[1] Bryant (2005a, p. 9).

Defense Research Institute, a federally funded research and development center sponsored by the Office of the Secretary of Defense, the Joint Staff, the Unified Combatant Commands, the Department of the Navy, the Marine Corps, the defense agencies, and the defense Intelligence Community.

For more information on RAND's International Security and Defense Policy Center, contact the Director, James Dobbins. He can be reached by email at James_Dobbins@rand.org; by phone at 703-413-1100, extension 5134; or by mail at RAND, 1200 South Hayes Street, Arlington, Virginia 22202-5050. More information about RAND is available at www.rand.org.

Contents

Figures

Summary

Background

Her Majesty's Australian Ship *Manoora* broke the horizon just as the first C-130 aircraft loaded with Regional Assistance Mission to Solomon Islands (RAMSI) personnel landed on July 24, 2003, at Henderson Field, the airport for that nation's capital, Honiara. The perfect timing was not accidental. It was meant to demonstrate to any who might consider resisting that RAMSI was a force to be reckoned with. Nor was the posture of the soldiers who exited the aircraft any less calculated. Armed, poised, and ready for any eventuality, they nonetheless waved to the many citizens happy to see the arrival of men and women who would free them from the threat of militias, criminals, and the violence that those groups had for years imposed on the innocent.

The years prior to the July 2003 arrival had seen tribal differences and simple criminal violence tear the islands' society apart. Ethnic antipathies and greed blossomed into violent atrocity in 1998. Militias, gangs, and an ever more corrupt police force (the Solomon Islands have no military) used rape, murder, theft, and destruction to intimidate opposition or achieve retribution. An International Peace Monitoring Team (IPMT) of 49 people from neighboring island nations proved unable to halt the violence permanently in 2000. Nor did elections in 2001 restore order and the rule of law. By 2003, the situation had deteriorated to the point that both the nation's Prime Minister Sir Allen Kemakeza and parliament members sought outside assistance. Five nations provided military capabilities; ten sent law enforcement officers. The force that arrived consisted of some 1,800 soldiers, fewer than 300 police personnel, and members of participant nations' foreign affairs organizations. Despite the relative numbers, it was Australia's senior Department of Foreign Affairs and Trade (DFAT) representative, Nick Warner, who was in overall charge. Police, not soldiers, dictated matters at the tactical level. In short, the army, navy, and air forces were in a supporting role at the tactical, operational, and strategic levels. Warner set policy and worked diligently to ensure a unity of message within and beyond the theater of operations. On the ground, RAMSI police conducted combined patrols with Solomon Islanders who were kept on the force. The mission's soldiers were also granted full powers of arrest. They never exercised the privilege as they protected the law enforcement officers, however, choosing to instead remain visible yet always in a supporting role. Any Solomon Islander approaching a soldier with a formal complaint was rerouted to a member of the Royal Solomon Islands Police (RSIP), and eventually it was the police to whom the people would once again have to turn in times of need, and it was thus the RSIP in which all members of RAMSI wanted to instill renewed public confidence.

RAMSI proceeded according to a three-phase plan. The first phase, *commencement*, was to last approximately six months. The objectives were to restore stability by disarming the population, reestablish law and order, capture militant leaders and criminals, and strengthen the police force. Phase two, *consolidation*, was to begin in January 2004 and end a year later. Emphasis would be on institutional reform: eliminating the corruption that ran rife through all aspects of the Solomon Islands government and training officials so that they could provide the services the citizens of the country so badly needed. The final phase, *sustainability and self-reliance*, was to start in January 2005. Its focus was the development of indigenous self-reliance and the solidification of governmental and social reforms.

RAMSI was initially funded through June 2008. However, Australia's Prime Minister John Howard, other participating nations' heads of government, and leaders at all echelons consistently emphasized that the mission was seen as a long-term one that would very likely extend well beyond that. Assistance would not cease until the nation had attained the end state collectively sought by its population, elected government officials, and members of RAMSI.

The many individuals interviewed in support of this study differed in their views regarding whether the pre-arrival situation in the Solomon Islands constituted an insurgency. Current doctrine and other readings regarding what constitutes an insurgency were often unhelpful. Most definitions, from U.S. and other sources, emphasize the political nature of insurgencies and require that the insurgents' ultimate goal be the replacement of a national government. Perhaps applicable to many insurgencies in the middle of the 20th century, this conceptualization is less helpful in the dawning years of the 21st and attendant insurgencies, which are at best superficially political and demonstrate little interest in governmental overthrow at a national level. As such, two alternative definitions serve the analysis here:

- *Insurgency*: an organized movement seeking to replace or undermine all or part of the sovereignty of one or more constituted governments through the protracted use of subversion and armed conflict[1]
- *Counterinsurgency*: an organized effort to preclude or defeat an insurgency.

Whether RAMSI confronted an insurgency, and was therefore a counterinsurgency undertaking, is addressed in the concluding pages of this study. That the mission was initially so successful and continues to be so—the occurrence of occasional demonstrations notwithstanding—makes it an undertaking worthy of study for anyone confronting or likely to confront stability operations of any character.

Three primary areas of notable performance underlie that success:

- effectively orchestrating interagency capabilities
- capitalizing on multinational resources
- gaining the moral and operational high ground.

---

[1]   The author thanks David Kilcullen for suggesting that the definition apply to "one or more" versus exclusively a single government (Kilcullen, 2006b).

Interagency Relationships, Multinational Cooperation, and Retaining the Moral and Operational High Ground

Interagency cooperation was exceptional despite the very short preparation time for RAMSI due to the limited duration between the decision to undertake the mission and deployment. Participants stressed a "whole of government" approach during planning and execution, one in which foreign affairs, police, military, aid agencies (several of which were already in the Solomon Islands at the time of deployment), and other organizations sought to capitalize on the synergies of mutual cooperation. The somewhat unusual command relationships between RAMSI forces and RSIP reflect a subordination of traditional methods (e.g., the agency with the greatest strength in theater leads) to ultimate ends sought. The cooperation among the initial "Big Three" representatives from the lead nation—the senior representatives from DFAT (Nick Warner), the Australian Federal Police (Ben McDevitt), and the Australian Defence Force (Lieutenant Colonel John Frewen)—exemplified a dedication to mission that permeated RAMSI at all echelons. This trio presented a unified face to Solomon Islanders, their own subordinates, and, with rare exceptions, Australia's capital, Canberra. They thus avoided internecine struggles and the related tensions that can undermine focus on the tasks at hand. The exceptional cooperation was maintained even as the military members rotated out of theater (their tours of duty being approximately four months while those of Warner and McDevitt were one year). Personalities played a significant part. They were characterized by a desire to emphasize the common good before individual or bureaucratic interests. The result was a striking achievement: unity of message and effort. This consistency allowed RAMSI to communicate its objectives through word and deed and to accomplish them with minimal disruption.

Similar teamwork exemplified the relationships between the ten participating nations' members in the multinational realm. Disagreements were kept to a minimum, as was largely the case in the interagency realm. National contingents were not assigned areas of responsibility. Units and individuals instead worked together to take advantage of cultural and language similarities and maintain consistent standards in police development, population interactions, and recovery assistance. Intelligence matters caused some early problems (as they did in the interagency relationships), but these frustrations were worked out over time. Cooperation among military personnel benefited from one advantage that was less evident in nonmilitary interactions. Many of the leaders of the five participating countries' armed forces had worked together during previous operations or international exchanges. These personal relationships and related common understanding of doctrine and professional language quickened the maturing of working relationships to the advantage of mission collaboration.

This willingness to work together was fundamental to taking the moral and operational high ground. The immediate objective—one served by the coordinated appearance of sea and air capabilities—was to demonstrate overwhelming force to communicate to militants the futility of resistance. At the same time, RAMSI's participants at every level remembered that it was the people they had come to serve: thus the deliberate portrayal of a capable-but-nonthreatening force, beginning with its exit from the aircraft at Henderson Field and its effort to ensure that there was a highly visible police patrol on the streets of Honiara the very afternoon of the mission's arrival, one with both Solomon Islander and RAMSI participation. There was no let-up in the reinforcement of the message that RAMSI was there to help and that it would not leave until the job was done. The Big Three maintained a routine of extensive travel from the start, visiting villages throughout the islands to communicate their messages to the people personally, explaining why RAMSI was in their country, what it would do for the population, what Solomon Islanders could do to assist in bringing about a better way of life, and willingly answering questions to address the inevitable misunderstandings and rumors that either arose inadvertently or were planted deliberately by foes of any counterinsurgency or other stability operation. Patrolling soldiers carried cards that emphasized one or two points that were currently most important to overall RAMSI objectives, the goal being consistency in public interactions throughout the islands. These messages were coordinated with the police so that military and law enforcement information was mutually supportive. Australian Prime Minister John Howard's declarations of intent to stay the course provided strategic reinforcement of the message at every echelon below, down to and including that of the police and soldiers on patrol. The messages, from on high or via the street, were kept simple and thus as free of misinterpretation or deliberate misconstruing as possible. The battlefields of counterinsurgency and stability operations are more often the human mind and social organizations than physical terrain. An intelligent enemy or other savvy group looks for seams between motivations. Interested parties seek to capitalize on bureaucratic jealousies and assail any available rift in their efforts to separate supposed allies, sow distrust in the population, or achieve other goals. An organization that tolerates such seams, or whose members put individual interests before collective ones, aids and abets the adversary it must eventually defeat to be successful. Nick Warner, Ben McDevitt, John Frewen, and those serving with and after them understood this. They were committed to minimizing the interagency, multinational, and other bureaucratic rifts through which divisiveness could seep and thereafter undermine mission success.

Common Elements

Several elements are common to the three foundational components of successful interagency, multinational, and shaping operations that proved so important to RAMSI and the welfare of the Solomon Islands' population. They offer lessons for COIN undertakings elsewhere:

- *Intelligence*: Effective, cooperative operations combined with an intolerance of intelligence empires facilitates the spread of information to those who can make best use of it.
- *Leadership*: From the highest to the lowest echelons, successful leadership requires selecting the right men and women for the challenge, to include ensuring that they understand the need to balance the use or threat of force with restraint. Americans deployed to Afghanistan and Iraq have described incidents in which members of newly arrived units expressed—verbally or through their actions—aggressiveness unsuited to their coun-

terinsurgency responsibilities. RAMSI personnel employed the threat of force so successfully that they never had to engage a threat with the intention of wounding or killing.

- *Control*: Mission members worked closely alongside government officials rather than replacing them outright, a key factor in rebuilding and maintaining Solomon Islands governmental legitimacy. Residents were always governed by their own leaders while RAMSI personnel assumed the roles of advisors and providers of assistance rather than that of occupiers. RAMSI did not replace the rule of law with one of its own making; it returned to that existent before societal breakdown. These and other actions reduced any potential conceptions of the international force as an occupying one. Yet mission leaders wisely kept control of the ultimate lever in a government reliant on graft: its funding. They also sought to ensure that those abusing the system most heinously were removed while others with promise were given the opportunity to change their ways. As the security situation improved, the mission executed a smooth and effective transition, increasing emphasis on aid, eradicating corruption, and bolstering Solomon Islanders' self-sufficiency while reducing the number of personnel whose primary purpose was security maintenance.

- *Focus on the people*: The Big Three and their subordinates never lost sight of their primary concern despite the early priorities of disarmament and militia leader arrest: the welfare of the Solomon Islands citizenry and the essential support they offered the mission. The people supported RAMSI from the moment of arrival. None in the mission took the support for granted. There was no end to the "honeymoon period" because the good will was never permitted to lapse. The result was a continually supportive population, one whose faith and confidence in the foreigners and their promises increased as time passed. They did not turn against RAMSI as seeming occupiers. They increasingly become providers of intelligence and a collective mouthpiece that further disseminated RAMSI messages as confidence grew.

Additional Elements Underlying RAMSI's Success

There are underlying reasons why RAMSI has been and continues to be successful in meeting the challenges related to interagency and multinational operations, maintaining the moral and operational high ground, and otherwise addressing its objectives. Despite the difference in scale, the nature of the foe, and other conditions, many of the reasons for RAMSI's success apply to ongoing activities in Iraq and Afghanistan, and have pertinence for future counterinsurgency and other stability operations. Key elements in this regard include

- Collocation of key personalities and staff sections, the appointment of able and qualified liaison officers in sufficient numbers, and intolerance of personal and bureaucratic agendas are all hallmarks of RAMSI. The existence of a single point of contact in Canberra through which all issues are routed ensures that those on the ground in the Solomon Islands have a champion in the hallways of the lead nation's capital. Misunderstandings regarding various agency planning methods or staff procedures sometimes hindered RAMSI's effectiveness, but its members adapted and continue to adapt. They seek to institute academic and operational exchanges of personnel to reduce the likelihood of such issues during future RAMSI rotations or other operations. It is notable that U.S. Department of Defense schools and doctrine writers are incorporating lessons from Afghanistan and Iraq into curriculums and manuals more quickly and more effectively than ever before. There has been notably less progress in advancing interagency coordination and understanding or exchanges with nations emerging as those most crucial to future U.S. interests.
- RAMSI police and military personnel alike found many familiar faces among those from other nations as they prepared to deploy. That is, in part, explained by the number of recent regional operations in the southwest Pacific. It is also reflective of the commitment to developing professional exchanges that later can provide such payoff. Similar U.S. exchanges, with other agencies as well as nations, should favor those nations with which it is most likely

to work in future coalitions rather than traditional relationships more reminiscent of Cold War–era relations than reflective of current operations. (The two are not always mutually exclusive, the relationship with the United Kingdom, Australia, and New Zealand being prime examples.) Personnel records should identify those who shared seminars with, sponsored, or otherwise established relationships with international or other agency representatives. (U.S. armed forces personnel files already include notations regarding international military exchange tours.)

- The presumption that each nation be assigned its own area of responsibility during operations merits reconsideration. Mission objectives might at times be better served were other agency, military, or indigenous personnel integrated with organizations on an individual or small-group basis rather than creating separate fiefdoms. The U.S.–Republic of Korea program for Korean Augmentation to the United States Army (KATUSA) potentially offers lessons in this regard.
- Unit leaders in the Solomon Islands reined in their soldiers' and their own aggressive tendencies; they exercised patience without dulling the sharpness of organizational performance. These observations beg the question of whether the same qualities of leadership so appreciated in combat are best suited for counterinsurgency undertakings in which an enemy is of secondary rather than primary importance.
- Governmental aid representatives stayed the course during even the worst of the violence, then integrated themselves into the frequent meetings chaired by the Big Three—the better to orchestrate RAMSI's diplomatic, police, military, and assistance capabilities. That such unity of message and effort has continued despite the transition from a mission dominated by security concerns to an aid-centric one speaks to the common dedication of leaders from all functional areas.
- The interagency cooperation, orchestration of multinational talents, and maintenance of unity of message that were so important in RAMSI's first years are equally important now. They will remain so during the years of commitment that lie ahead. Partici-

pating nations' leaders understand that diligence in selecting the right personnel for deployment and appointing others who support RAMSI within their governments is as vital now as it was in summer 2003.

- RAMSI has always been envisioned as a long-term commitment that will take years, perhaps decades. Consistency of support for this understanding ensures that Solomon Islanders are comfortable with continuing to demonstrate their support for change and that they need not fear for their welfare. They are confident that RAMSI will not abandon the country and its citizens.

Conclusion

Consideration of the challenges facing RAMSI in light of the proposed broader definition of insurgency results in the conclusion that the operation's members may well have encountered a nascent insurgency on arrival. The evidence supports a conclusion that, if this is so, RAMSI's operations interdicted the insurgency in its first stage, during a time when mission was just developing and when it was most vulnerable.

RAMSI leaders and those supporting them from participating nations' capitals consciously maintained consistency of purpose, control of the operational environment, and dedication to a long-term commitment. The success of RAMSI owes much to these accomplishments, achievements that compare favorably with those of any operation in history. Unity of message, unity of effort, a focus on the population, a steady input of quality leadership: these and other factors so crucial to controlling the situation in the theater all rely on the interagency and multinational cooperation and the retention of the moral and operational high ground that have been hallmarks of the mission. Control has not been perfect. The Solomon Islands are not a laboratory in which RAMSI participants can influence every factor in the manner desired. Yet they have been sufficiently successful that RAMSI stands as a sterling example of success in interdicting an insurgency and moving toward a stable and secure nation in the South Pacific.

Acknowledgments

This study owes its existence to the many men and women who self-lessly offered their time and wisdom during interview sessions conducted in Australia and New Zealand during the month of November 2005 and the several who did so in 2003. Their names appear in the bibliography. The author sincerely thanks each and every one of them; he is especially appreciative of those who further assisted by helping to arrange further interviews or subsequently provided input on early drafts.

A special thanks is due to Lieutenant Colonel Jim Bryant. This Australian Army officer was working on his own RAMSI study during the time that I was conducting research. He offered both insights and a draft of his notable effort, and continued to assist during my own writing by answering questions and reviewing an early version of this study. Similar appreciation is due the New Zealand Army's Lieutenant Colonel John Howard for his most valuable gift of resources in addition to personal insights, and to that nation's Group Captain Shaun Clarke and his family for the extraordinary professional and personal hospitality.

Few are the RAND Corporation documents that do not owe much of their pith and polish, if not their very existence, to hidden heroines and heroes: the administrative assistants, librarians, editors, and publications managers who take an author's work and create a product suitable for public scrutiny. Gayle Stephenson, my administrative assistant, typed tens of thousands of words for notes and was otherwise fundamental to this document's creation. Librarian Judy Lesso—sadly no longer with RAND—never failed to support an information request; it was thanks to her that I went to Australia and New Zealand with an initial understanding of the challenges RAMSI presented to all participants and of the suffering endured by Solomon Islands citizens. Lauren Skrabala was both artful and quick as editor, a perfect combination for which I am very grateful.

Finally, I was exceptionally fortunate in having two truly outstanding professionals formally review this document. James T. Quinlivan and David J. Kilcullen provided perceptive insights and expansions on other materials that substantially enhanced this publication.

Abbreviations

2RAR	2nd Battalian, The Royal Australian Regiment
3RAR	3rd Battalion, The Royal Australian Regiment
ABCI	Australian Federal Police Bureau of Criminal Intelligence
ADF	Australian Defence Force
ALO	air liaison officer
AFP	Australian Federal Police
AO	area of operation
APS	Australian Protective Service
AQIS	Australian Quarantine Inspection Service
AusAID	Australian Agency for International Development
BATT 3	3rd Battalion, New Zealand Army
BRA	Bougainville Revolutionary Army
C2	command and control
C2X	coalition intelligence staff section, counterintelligence and human intelligence
CFLCC	Coalition Forces Land Component Command
CIA	Central Intelligence Agency

CIMIC	civil-military coordination
CJTF	Coalition Joint Task Force
COIN	counterinsurgency
CPA	Coalition Provisional Authority
CSS	combat service support
CTF	Combined Task Force
DFAT	Australia Department of Foreign Affairs and Trade
DRN	Defence Restricted Network
DSN	Defence Secret Network
EW	electronic warfare
FARC	Fuerzas Armadas Revolucionarias de Colombia (Revolutionary Armed Forces of Colombia)
GLF	Guadalcanal Liberation Force
HQ	headquarters
HUMINT	human intelligence
ICRC	International Committee of the Red Cross
IDC	interdepartmental committee
IFM	Isatabu Freedom Movement
INTERFET	International Force in East Timor
IO	information operations
IPMT	International Peace Monitoring Team
IRA	Irish Republican Army
ISE	intelligence support element
J1	personnel staff section in a joint headquarters

J2	intelligence staff section in a joint headquarters
J3	training and operations staff section in a joint headquarters
J4	logistics staff section in a joint headquarters
J5	plans staff section in a joint headquarters
J6	communications staff section in a joint headquarters
J7	engineering staff section in a joint headquarters
JLM	joint land maneuver
KATUSA	Korean Augmentation to the United States Army
LCH	landing craft–heavy
LCM8	landing craft–medium, model 8
LOG	logistics
MEF	Malaitan Eagle Force
MGI	military geographic information
MILAD	military advisor
MP	military police
MWV	minor war vessel (e.g., a patrol boat or LCH)
NGO	nongovernmental organization
NZAID	New Zealand's International Aid and Development Agency
OfOf	orders for opening fire
OPCON	operational control
ORHA	Office of Reconstruction and Humanitarian Assistance
PA	public affairs

PIC	Pacific Islands Contingent
PMG	Peace Monitoring Group
PNG	Papua New Guinea
PNGDF	Papua New Guinea Defence Force
PPF	participating police forces
PSYOP	psychological operations
RAAF	Royal Australian Air Force
RAAF ELM	Royal Australian Air Force element
RACMP	Royal Australian Corps of Military Police
RAMSI	Regional Assistance Mission to Solomon Islands
RAN	Royal Australian Navy
RAN LO	Royal Australian Navy liaison officer
ROE	rules of engagement
RSIP	Royal Solomon Islands Police
SIG SQN	signal squadron
SIGS	signals
SIPRNET	Secret Internet Protocol Router Network
SOLO	special operations liaison officer
SPPKF	South Pacific Peace-Keeping Force
STAR	Special Task and Rescue Division
TERM	terminal detachment
TMG	Truce Monitoring Group
TNI	Tentara Nasional Indonesia [Indonesian armed forces]
TPA	Townsville Peace Agreement

UAV	unmanned aerial vehicle
UHIH	model of helicopter
UNAMET	United Nations Mission in East Timor
UNTAET	United Nations Transitional Administration in East Timor
USMC	U.S. Marine Corps

CHAPTER ONE

Background and Brief History of Operation Helpem Fren, the Regional Assistance Mission to Solomon Islands (RAMSI)

The great point to aim at is not so much that there should be no delay in getting into motion, as that when once in motion there should be no check. An ephemeral triumph is dearly purchased at the cost of a subsequent period of discreditable inaction.

For it is a cardinal principle in the conduct of warfare of this nature that the initiative must be maintained, that the regular army must lead while its adversaries follow, and that the enemy must be made to feel a moral inferiority throughout.
>   —*Colonel C. E. Callwell ([1906] 1976)*

The conduct of internal-security operations from Ireland to Malaya was based not on formal doctrine but on three broad principles deeply ingrained in the thinking of British soldiers and colonial civil servants. First, English common law dictated that disorders had to be suppressed with minimum force. . . . Second, successful counterinsurgency depended on close co-operation between all branches of the civil government and the military. . . . Third, the military for its part had to dispense with conventional tactics and adopt a highly decentralized, small-unit approach to combating irregulars.
>   —*Thomas R. Mockaitis (1990)*

Previous Operations

Many of the nations supporting RAMSI—formally designated Operation Helpem Fren ("Helping Friend" in Solomon Islands pidgin)—benefited from their men and women's experiences in other missions around the world in the years preceding the July 24, 2003, arrival of the coalition in the Solomon Islands. Operations in Cambodia, Somalia, Rwanda, Papua New Guinea, East Timor, and elsewhere all involved one or more RAMSI member nation. Those actions provided lessons that would serve the participants in good stead in the Solomon Islands, but they also provided experiences that were unfortunately overlooked in that undertaking. A brief look at two of these earlier operations assists in providing insights in this regard: those on Papua New Guinea's Bougainville Island and in East Timor.

Bougainville

Secessionists attempted to separate the southern Pacific island of Bougainville's government from the remainder of Papua New Guinea (PNG) even before the latter gained independence from Australia in 1975.[1] (See Figure 1.1.) Though forestalled at that point, the underlying causes of discontent—land disputes prompted by the PNG government's allowing the development of copper and gold mining on Bougainville, an accompanying influx of workers from other areas, and related environmental problems, among others—festered in subsequent years. Disagreements over the mining operations spurred the initial violence in 1969 and again underlay that in 1988, violence that by 1990 devolved into regular clashes between PNG constabulary and military forces and the separatist Bougainville Revolutionary Army (BRA), violence that included atrocities by both sides. The opposing factions eventually agreed to a peace conference in September 1994. Some 400 soldiers from the neighboring island nations of Australia, New Zealand, Vanuatu, Tonga, and Fiji comprised the South Pacific Peace-Keeping Force (SPPKF) that was to guarantee the safety of

---

[1] Peter Londey (2004, p. 215). The summary here relies on Londey (2004, pp. 215–229) unless otherwise noted.

Figure 1.1
Bougainville and the South Pacific Ocean Region

West Pacific Islands

SOURCE: Map courtesy of the University of Texas Libraries,
The University of Texas at Austin.
RAND MG551-1.1

conference attendees. Australia and New Zealand provided special forces, amphibious capability, air and sea transport, and logistical support; the former also providing the force commander. Planning problems and a timetable rushed for political reasons resulted in only a week of training for the SPPKF force and its arrival but two days before the event.

The mission was a limited one: "To provide a secure environment for the conduct of the Bougainville Peace Conference, and to provide security and movement for selected delegates." Rules of engagement significantly constrained the force's ability to accomplish even these narrow objectives. While SPPKF soldiers could use force to defend conference attendees and themselves, they were prohibited from detaining individuals conducting suspicious activity in the vicinity of the event. Further, there was no guidance regarding whether the SPPKF had the right to confiscate weapons within the neutral zones delineated at and nearby the conference site. Operations were further hindered in that the size of the force was insufficient to ensure the security of its assigned areas of responsibility. Criminals moved into those areas declared neutral and thus evacuated by the Papua New Guinea Defence Force (PNGDF), further burdening an SPPKF responsible for that terrain. Elsewhere, PNGDF soldiers who did not support the peace effort attacked delegates and members of the SPPKF. Politics also complicated the mission; Australia's role was resented by separatists who believed that the country's neutrality had been compromised by the training, equipment, and operational support that its military had provided the PNGDF (including helicopter gun ships used against the BRA). These many factors conspired to precipitate mission failure. Secessionist leaders chose not to attend out of fear that the SPPKF would be unable to ensure their safety. The multinational force, the first ever led by the Australian military, departed Bougainville less than two weeks after its arrival.

Continued violence in the aftermath of the aborted 1994 meetings resulted in renewed international efforts to foster resolution. A July 1997 truce agreement provided for "a neutral regional group" to monitor a ceasefire. New Zealand took command of the Truce Monitoring Group (TMG) after some initial resistance by Australia, other parties having convinced the Australians that their previous status as a colonial power undermined local perceptions of neutrality. Half of the resulting force was from New Zealand. Soldiers from Fiji, civilians from Vanuatu, and logistical personnel and civilian truce monitors from Australia completed the commitment.

TMG participants were to be unarmed, much to the discomfort of many participants. There were several reasons for this decision. It was felt that the small number of TMG members called into question the wisdom of employing armed resistance against any significant attacks. Further, the lack evident TMG arms meant that there was no temptation to assault monitoring group representatives in the interest of stealing their weapons. There were those who believed that wounding or killing any Bougainvillean would have fundamentally undermined the operation itself. Finally, TMG weapons might have served as a counterproductive example, as arms were a significant part of the island's problems and disarming the competing factions was a primary goal of the peace initiative.[2]

Multinational monitoring teams quickly established a routine of traveling throughout the island to inform villagers about the peace process. Building favorable relations with the population required considerable patience. Meetings were long and often accompanied by meals, sports, and entertainment, keeping with Melanesian custom. TMG member perseverance was mixed with demonstrations of humanitarian concern, such as the provision of medical care and assistance in transporting local civilians over the harsh terrain. The patience paid off. Cooperation with and support for the peace process were substantial. This success during local meetings had a higher-echelon counterpart wherein the former combatant parties were brought together in negotiations and problem-solving sessions.

The preparation of those assigned to later TMG rotations took advantage of earlier participants' experiences. Subsequent deployments included increased numbers of women, for example, their presence having been found to better facilitate relations with Bougainville's female population. The lessons also influenced actions taken to better participants' general readiness for deployments. New Zealand found that a lack of staff coordination between those responsible for TMG strategic and operational planning interfered with their operations in the theater. The nation's armed forces subsequently adapted their approach to emulate that used by the Australian Defence Force (ADF).

A Peace Monitoring Group (PMG) replaced the TMG in April 1998. Australia now assumed the leadership role, with the senior nego-

---

[2] Noble (2006).

tiators including a New Zealand officer and a representative of Australia's Department of Foreign Affairs and Trade.[3] By this time the warring parties had agreed to a "permanent and irrevocable" ceasefire. The primary emphasis gradually changed over a period of several years from monitoring security to development. Maintenance of good relations with Bougainville's population remained a high priority. Women continued to play a vital role, as did Fiji, Vanuatu, New Zealand Maori, and Australian Aborigine monitors whose cultures shared elements with Bougainville Melanesians. In August 2001, an agreement providing for the islands' autonomy and generally improved living conditions allowed for the eventual departure of the PMG in June 2003.

The implications of the Bougainville operations extended beyond the borders of the island and the mission's end date. A generation of Australian, Pacific Islander, and New Zealand police, diplomats, and military personnel gained experience and built relationships that would serve them well when they once again found themselves working together. Many of these same individuals would be in senior leadership positions by the time RAMSI occurred, providing a well-established basis for close interagency cooperation.[4]

East Timor

East Timor (now Timor-Leste) was an unfortunate victim of the colonial era's worst practices and their resultant consequences. It was poorly administered by Portugal, left ill prepared for self-governing, and it devolved into civil war in the aftermath of Portugal's withdrawal in 1974. After an extended period of instability, it was eventually invaded by Indonesia though neighboring West Timor.[5] (See Figure 1.2.) Insurgent resistance against the Indonesian occupation was gradually suppressed by the early 1990s, but periodic conflict occasionally flared anew, supported by Timorese diaspora groups supporting independence. These tensions burned to the surface once again in early 1999

---

[3] Kilcullen (2006b).

[4] Kilcullen (2006b).

[5] The material in this section is drawn from the following sources unless otherwise noted: Londey (2004), Ryan (2000), and Crawford and Harper (2001).

when the new Habibie government announced that East Timor would vote on independence from Indonesia following the fall of the Suharto government that had previously maintained rigid control over the territory. Militia groups, recruited and sometimes led by intelligence and special forces units from the Indonesian armed forces (the Tentara Nasional Indonesia, or TNI), stormed through communities, massacring and deporting inhabitants and razing buildings. The United Nations Mission in East Timor (UNAMET), which had been dispatched to monitor the referendum process, soon found itself under severe pressure. UNAMET was a police-heavy force augmented by military and civilian personnel. Its challenges were reminiscent of those of the earlier SPPKF in Bougainville. Like the SPPKF, UNAMET had very limited powers and too few numbers given the nature of the threat at hand. It had no powers of arrest; its members were unarmed and frustrated as they witnessed militia attacks on innocent civilians, attacks unimpeded by the TNI. Despite the militia violence, 98.6 percent

Figure 1.2
East Timor and Its Region

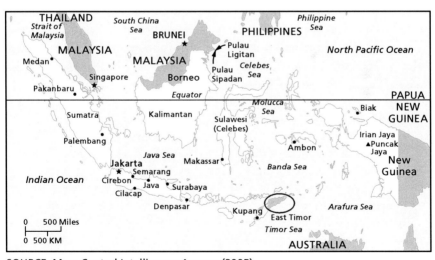

SOURCE: Map, Central Intelligence Agency (2005).
RAND *MG551-1.2*

of East Timor's registered voters took part in the elections held on August 30, 1999, 78 percent of whom favored independence with their ballots. The militia sensed the outcome even before the results were formally announced. Further rampages began on September 4, resulting in the killing of many Timorese and two UNAMET members. The organization thereafter evacuated most of its force, leaving its equipment behind. The few who remained moved into the almost deserted Australian consulate located in the capital city, Dili.

The international community reacted quickly to the depredations. On September 15, the United Nations Security Council authorized the creation of a military force that would come to be known as International Force East Timor (INTERFET). It was intended to "restore peace and security," support UNAMET efforts, and facilitate humanitarian assistance. Australia led the Chapter VII peacekeeping operations, the first time in its history it had undertaken the task under those auspices. It was also the largest peacekeeping effort in which the nation had ever participated. A total of 22 nations would eventually support the effort, a force that included infantry units from New Zealand, Jordan, South Korea, Canada, the United Kingdom, Fiji, Italy, and Kenya, in addition to those from the lead nation, as well as extensive U.S. logistical support. Much went well. Nevertheless, the Australians found that multinational leadership imposed unfamiliar responsibilities. Historian Peter Londey addressed some of these in his *Other People's Wars: A History of Australian Peacekeeping*:

> It was not all perfect. Interfet headquarters was heavily dominated by Australians, with the result that other national contingents could feel left out. Australia provided liaison officers to work with the other national contingents, but they rarely spoke the relevant language or were familiar with the contingent's culture. The language problems were exacerbated by other nationals' difficulty in understanding the Australian accent and by the Australian habit of delivering jargon-filled briefings rapidly and laconically, with limited regard for listeners for whom English was not their native language. Even New Zealanders found the headquarters at times arrogantly Australian and unwilling to consult. Other cultural differences caused friction. Many coalition partners found

the Australian soldiers overly aggressive, with their weapons constantly at the ready and wearing dark glasses which prevented eye contact.[6]

It was another echo from Bougainville: During those operations there had been complaints about Australian and New Zealand arrogance from some of the other national contingents. Despite the rough spots and misunderstandings, participation by the many countries' participants added substantively to INTERFET's efforts. There was occasionally room for improvement on their part as well. Australia's Major General Duncan Lewis thought highly of the Republic of Korea's special forces unit in East Timor, for example, but others thought them "casualty paranoid."[7] Nations came with varying degrees of ability to sustain their numbers; the South Koreans were notably good in this regard as were members of the Thai military.[8] Adaptations were the norm as incoming units took advantage of predecessors' experiences, much as had been the case in Bougainville. Some of these lessons would have further benefit in the Solomon Islands. Australian observers noted, for example, that the visible presence of the U.S. Navy's USS *Belleau Wood* offshore made a significant impression on Indonesian army forces on Timor.[9]

Australian Major General Peter Cosgrove led INTERFET, first consolidating his force's position in Dili and later expanding its influence throughout the rest of the half-island and enclave of Oecusse, separated from the rest of East Timor by Indonesian West Timorese territory. (See Figure 1.3. Oecusse is the area surrounding Pante Makasar.) Though criticized in some quarters for moving too slowly given continued militia transgressions, Cosgrove ensured that his force secured Dili, its airport, and port, and that it was sufficiently well organized before extending its reach. Certain hot spots were at especially high-risk for armed clashes between INTERFET forces and those from the Indo-

---

[6] Londey (2004, p. 255).

[7] Lewis (2003).

[8] Houston (2003).

[9] Evans (2003).

nesian army. The soldiers of Lieutenant Colonel Peter Singh's 3rd Battalion, The Royal Australian Regiment (3RAR), for example, had only 10 meters between their positions and those of the Indonesian Army in some locations along the East Timor–West Timor border. Shouting matches between the two sides threatened to evolve into more serious exchanges until Singh withdrew his men 100 meters to increase the buffer zone; his counterpart did the same.[10]

INTERFET and remaining UNAMET personnel—military, police, and civilian alike—immediately set to work establishing favorable relations with the indigenous population. Singh's personnel taught arithmetic to the citizenry in the 3RAR area of operations; the locals provided language instruction in return and helped the Australians

Figure 1.3
East Timor

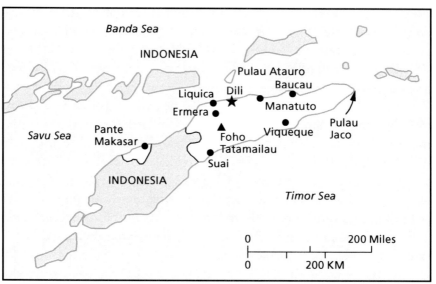

SOURCE: Central Intelligence Agency (2005).
RAND MG551-1.3

---

[10] Singh (2003).

distinguish between fact and rumor in their interactions with the populace, not an inconsequential contribution in the tumultuous social environment.[11] Dramatically improved intelligence was one of the many benefits. The unofficial motto of the 3rd Battalion, New Zealand Army (BATT 3), reflected the importance of the initiative: "Better 100,000 pairs of eyes than just our 700."[12] The observation was all the more applicable given that humanitarian and relationship-building endeavors suffered continued militia attacks.[13]

United Nations Transitional Administration in East Timor (UNTAET) replaced UNAMET and INTERFET on October 25, 1999, under the auspices of a United Nations Security Council resolution.[14] UNTAET was a multinational, interagency force with civil governance, military, and police personnel totaling in excess of 10,000. It was granted legislative and executive powers to organize and oversee the full scope of East Timor's transition to statehood. Sergio Vieira de Mello, who would die in the 2003 bombing of the United Nations headquarters bombing in Iraq, was its senior representative. General Cosgrove formally handed over security responsibilities to UNTAET on February 23, 2000.

RAMSI: A Concise History

> The first requirement for a workable campaign is good coordinating machinery. It is no good having an overall plan composed of various measures unless they can be coordinated in such a way that measures of one kind do not cut across measures of another kind.
>
> —*Frank Kitson (1977)*

---

[11] Singh (2003).

[12] Crawford and Harper (2001, p. 143).

[13] Singh (2003).

[14] McDonald (2001).

> We have some crusty old dinosaurs that aren't ready to change. . . .
> Instead of saying, "Here's your mission and get on with it," [they
> have to oversee every action.] . . . We are getting there slowly but
> surely, but I'd like to get there faster. It's getting better with new
> generations.
>
> —*Anonymous*

The Backdrop to RAMSI

The Solomon Islands gained their independence from the United Kingdom and became a member of the British Commonwealth in 1978.[15]
They are a nation with little arable land, their geography dominated by
mountainous and often densely vegetated terrain. The country's strategic location along the sea routes between the Coral Sea, the Solomon
Sea, and the south Pacific Ocean was a significant factor in the inva-
sion and seizure of its Guadalcanal Island from Japanese occupiers by
the U.S. Marine Corps (USMC) during World War II. (See Figure 1.4
for a map of the Solomon Islands and neighboring nations.)

The Solomon Islands' 2004 estimated population was 523,167,
a number that continues to increase sharply due to a high birth rate
of 30.01 births per 1,000 people.[16] The largely Christian population is approximately 95-percent Melanesian. Over 80 percent of the
nation's citizenry depends on subsistence agriculture or fishing; many
of them reside in remote villages accessible only from the sea, air, or
after extended travel over tortuous land routes often traversable only by
foot or beast of burden.[17] The capital city, Honiara, is home to approximately 50,000 Solomon Islanders and the nation's parliamentary
democratic government.[18] That government and the nation's society in

---

[15] The geographic and demographic information for this overview is taken from Central
Intelligence Agency (2006), unless otherwise noted.

[16] Population estimate from Central Intelligence Agency (2006).

[17] Subsistence agriculture datum from Australian Agency for International Development
(2006a, p. 2).

[18] The population estimate for Honiara is based on a 1999 value; significant turmoil since
then makes the estimate at best an approximate one.

Figure 1.4
Solomon Islands and Environs

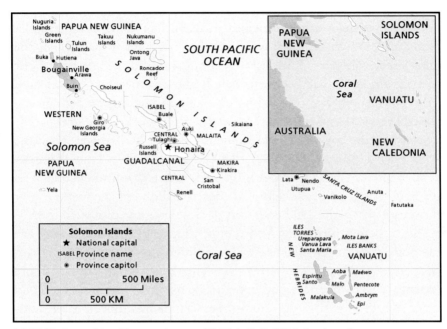

SOURCE: Central Intelligence Agency (1989) in ReliefWeb (undated).
RAND MG551-1.4

general has been frequently torn by factionalism and instability since independence, a factor that severely impacted economic development and dramatically reduced primary product exports (in the mining, copra, fishing, and palm oil industries).[19] The continued unrest and related lack of investment has contributed to significant lead, zinc, and gold resources going largely untapped.

The Royal Solomon Islands Police is the country's police force; the nation has no military. English, the official language, is spoken by merely 1 to 2 percent of the population. Many citizens speak Melanesian pidgin, but there are 63 distinct languages indigenous to the islands and many local dialects.[20] The literacy rate is low, as is access

---

[19] Australian Agency for International Development (2006a, p. 1).

[20] Australian Department of Foreign Affairs and Trade (2006).

to primary and secondary education in comparison to other Pacific countries.[21]

Many of those supporting RAMSI drew on the lessons of those with experiences during previous missions in Bougainville, East Timor, and elsewhere. They were not the only ones to partake of the region's recent history. Nearly 9,000 Bougainvilleans had crossed the short expanse of water between their island and nearby Guadalcanal to escape the civil war. According to a United Nations report, "it was inevitable that they would have shared with [the] Guadalcanal people information on how they (the Bougainvilleans) had driven away the Papua New Guinean Highlanders who had arrived in large numbers to staff a giant open-cut copper mine and assumed prominence in local business. Bougainvilleans had also confronted one of the world's largest mining companies and caused it to close its mine and withdraw."[22] Passage of such information boded poorly for peace and stability in the Solomon Islands. Tensions were already high before Bougainvilleans' arrival due to disagreements between Guadalcanal natives and those residents whose ancestors had come from neighboring Malaita Island during World War II. Many from other islands had moved to Guadalcanal during and after the war, drawn by the greater economic opportunities presented by USMC installations on the island, and later by expansion in the palm oil industry. Honiara had grown up outside the main marine installation in the 1940s and matured into the Solomon Islands' most developed area. It became the colony's capital in 1953 and the national capital in 1978 upon independence.[23] Natives of Guadalcanal ("Gwales") and the nearby island of Malaita (Malaitans) had no antipathies of sufficient concern to interfere with cooperation in these early postwar years. The groups intermarried, Malaitans coming to fill many of the police and governmental positions in the colonial and, later, the national government.[24]

---

[21] Australian Agency for International Development (2006b).

[22] Office of the United Nations Resident Coordinator, United Nations Development Programme, (2002, p. 58).

[23] Watson (2005a, pp. 6–8).

[24] Frewen (2005b).

Unfortunately the passage of time had unsettling effects. By the late 1990s, the palm oil industry alone employed approximately 8,000 persons rather than the 400 only a quarter century before, resulting in further immigration from other islands.[25] In addition, inheritance customs of the two largest groups, Gwales and Malaitans, differed in that the former passed land from generation to generation through maternal lines (as did most of the islands' many tribes) while Malaitans favored a patrilineal policy. Gwales grew increasingly disgruntled as they lost traditional land holdings to Malaitans through intermarriage and outright purchase.[26] They also believed that they were not being justly compensated for government and private-company use of island territory.[27] In 1998, Guadalcanal finally saw the eruption of widespread organized violence. Frustrated members of its native population formed the Isatabu Freedom Movement (IFM) and other militia groups, later to include the Guadalcanal Liberation Force (GLF) that would compete with the IFM for control of areas in the island's Weathercoast (or Weather Coast) region. (See Figure 1.5.) These and other militia organizations ranged from fairly well-trained and disciplined forces to groups that were little more than gangs bent on thuggery.[28] Their members regularly committed atrocities, including murder, rape, theft, and destruction of property. Several of the worst groups on Guadalcanal focused on intimidating Malaitans.[29] Estimates of the number who resultantly fled back to their home island with the assistance of the International Committee of the Red Cross (ICRC)

---

[25] Watson (2005a, p. 7).

[26] Byant (2005a, p. 4).

[27] Fry (2000, p. 302).

[28] "There was an extensive history of trans-island criminal activity, including smuggling of weapons during the Bougainville conflict, particularly by inhabitants of the Shortland Archipelago, the part of the Solomons closest to Bougainville. Corruption and criminal activity associated with this clandestine 'war trade' were key factors in the [later] breakdown of stability in the Solomons" (Kilcullen, 2006b).

[29] Watson (2005a, pp. 7–8). The native Gwales were primarily members of the Isatabu tribe.

Figure 1.5
Guadalcanal Island and the Weathercoast Region

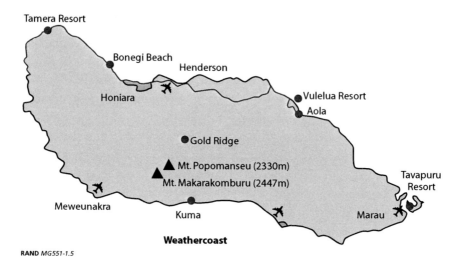

generally range from 10,000 to 20,000.[30] Others went to Honiara, where the Malaitan Eagle Force (MEF), a predominantly Malaitan militia, controlled a virtual enclave on the island. The MEF had formed in early 2000 as a response to the outbreak of Gwale-inspired violence, but it also wreaked violence on residents across the water on Malaita.[31] The MEF included many members of the Malaitan-dominated Royal Solomon Islands Police (RSIP) who provided them with quality weapons from police armories (a notable resource given that the Solomon Islands have no army).[32] Negotiation efforts headed by Commonwealth Secretariat representative Ade Afuye of Nigeria eventually precipitated a regional police agreement, the result of which was the arrival on

---

[30] Other estimates are higher. Hegarty (2001, p. 1) cites "the displacement of some 30,000 people," though he might be including those who moved between locations on Guadalcanal itself. Fraenkel (2003, p. 7) wrote that "by mid-1999, an estimated 35,309 people (58.6% of the Guadalcanal population) had been displaced," though here also the number may include internal movement on the island.

[31] Fry (2000, p. 300).

[32] Watson (2005a, p. 8).

Guadalcanal of a combined Fijian and Vanuatu police force with an intent to stop the lawlessness and violence.[33] The effort unsurprisingly failed given that it was inadequately resourced and lacked sufficient authority, much as had the initial efforts in Bougainville and East Timor.

The turmoil and associated suffering continued unabated. It became increasingly evident that there were close ties between Honiara's Malaitan politicians, the RSIP, local criminals, and militia members.[34] A coup in June 2000 precipitated the withdrawal of most remaining international investment and other nations' citizenry.[35] Killings in Honiara escalated sharply as the MEF formally declared war on the IFM. The island and the nation were on the cusp of total civil war.[36]

A ceasefire agreement temporarily interrupted the downslide. The Australian government, having been asked for assistance twice previously by the now-deposed prime minister, sent military forces to secure an area where the warring factions could meet. An August 2, 2000, a ceasefire set the preconditions for peace negotiations in Townsville, Australia, the following October. The result of those consultations was the Townsville Peace Agreement (TPA), a provision of which was the creation of an IPMT that was to oversee disarmament of the opposing factions. Militia members adhering to the agreement were to gain immunity from both criminal proceedings and civil liability in exchange for their cooperation. Some participants refused to be party to the immunity arrangement, a decision that later exposed them to prosecution that they might have otherwise avoided.[37]

---

[33] Anonymous interview.

[34] Anonymous interview.

[35] Bryant (2005a, pp. 4–5). Just as the UN believed that the influx of Bougainville's refugees from that island's civil war may have influenced the instability on Guadalcanal, the June 5, 2000, kidnapping of the Solomon Islands Prime Minister Bartholomew Ulufa'alu that initiated the coup was labeled a "copycat" coup by some members of the international media. Only two weeks earlier, an armed group headed by George Speight had taken members of Fiji's Chaudhry government hostage. (See Fry, 2000, p. 295.)

[36] Watson (2005a, p. 10).

[37] Watson (2005a, pp. 11–12); Bryant (2005a, p. 5).

The IPMT consisted of 49 police, military, and civilian personnel from several regional nations when it deployed in late 2000.[38] The organization's mandate and authority was limited, as were its accomplishments; only 150 of some 1,300 firearms turned in were of military quality. Once again, insufficient staffing and too little authority precluded attainment of a peace initiative's objectives. Corrupt Solomon Islands politicians, militia commanders, and other leaders pocketed the money that was to go to those turning in firearms.[39] Handovers stopped when those with weapons saw public officials taking what was rightfully meant for them. There was also only limited progress toward other objectives agreed to in the Townsville Peace Agreement prior to the IPMT's June 25, 2002, departure.[40]

Violence continued at unacceptable levels after the withdrawal of what many in retrospect called a "toothless tiger."[41] Yet, the IPMT mission was not without its benefits. Peter Noble, a New Zealander and deputy head of the operation, believed that the action conditioned the population to later involvement by external powers, thus setting

---

[38] Londey (2004, p. 226); Hegarty (2001).

[39] Noble (2006).

[40] Watson (2005a, p. 19).

[41] Bryant (2005a, p. 13). Kilcullen (2006b) argues that the heavy commitment of Australian and New Zealand forces to East Timor during the 2000–2002 time frame limited both the forces those countries could commit to another contingency and the extent to which the Solomon Islands crisis received attention in those nations' capitals. He also notes that the extent of concern in Canberra was influenced by warnings regarding the post–September 11, 2001, risks governmental collapse in the Solomons could precipitate, citing Wainwright (2003). Presenting a counter-perspective, Peter Noble argues that the term is

> a little harsh and a misappreciation often leveled at the IPMT. The reality was that the IPMT was a creation of the TPA and reflected "what the market would stand" by way of what the protagonists were prepared to allow. The context of the IPMT is often lost because of subsequent events. In essence the parties agreed to disarm and the IPMT was created to facilitate this process (subsequently subverted by the protagonists) and supervise the cantonment of the weapons. It took on confidence building and worked on maintaining/building attitudes against weapons in the community, which did later prove of use to RAMSI. In essence it became a bridging mission, as the blockage of its real mandate was realized early on. (Noble, 2006)

the stage for ready acceptance of RAMSI a year later.[42] As we will later see, James Watson, who provided legal counsel to RAMSI's military component, believed that the signing of the IPMT agreement was a hallmark in the neutralization of militia influence, as it established the legitimacy of external involvement to enforce the rule of law. It is also quite likely that the contrast in professionalism and honesty between Solomon Islands government representatives and members of the IPMT did not go unnoticed. Finally, the security team that had been ever present during the operation "provided a huge amount of information . . . for what was going to be the big show later on."[43]

The RSIP continued to be a source of violence and abuse rather than a protector of the people throughout 2002 and into 2003. The Malaitan-dominated government augmented the force with "special constables" after the 2000 coup.[44] The new component consisted primarily of MEF thugs who at first went by the name of Police Field Force and later the Special Task and Rescue Division (STAR).[45] Although democratic elections resulted in a new government in 2001, efforts to rein in interfactional violence and blatant police corruption required the nation's new prime minister, Albert Kamakeze, to request outside assistance once again in 2003.[46] (While the situation was bad, it could have been worse. Further problems were avoided when a $4 million weapons purchase arranged with the United States by a previous prime minister was interdicted, as were several ethically dubious interactions with Republic of Taiwan representatives.)[47] On July 21, 2003, the Solomon Islands parliament passed the Facilitation of International Assistance Act 2003 to back the prime minister's request for help. The act specified that the purpose of the now-pending international assistance operation was to "reinforce and uphold the legitimate institu-

---

[42] Noble (2005).

[43] Anonymous interview.

[44] Bryant (2005a, p. 5).

[45] Foster (2005).

[46] Bryant (2005a, p. 6).

[47] Bryant (2005a, p. 7); Fraenkel (2003, pp. 7–8).

tions and authorities in the Solomon Islands, and to ensure respect for the country's constitution and implementation of its laws."[48] The act included provisions to exempt members of an international peacekeeping force from prosecution or civil action under Solomon Islands law. It further granted them the right to use force when necessary and gave international police and military personnel the same powers granted the RSIP. Passage was timely. Three days later, on July 24, 2003, the first elements of RAMSI landed on Guadalcanal.[49] The military component, the Combined Task Force (CTF) 635, included elements of the 2nd Battalion, The Royal Australian Regiment (2RAR), and units from New Zealand, Fiji, PNG, and Tonga.[50] Police personnel included representatives of those five nations and others from Samoa, Vanuatu, Kiribati, the Cook Islands, and Nauru. The military element numbered 1,800, and the police 230; Australia's Department of Foreign Affairs and Trade (DFAT) initial leadership and entourage consisted of ten people.[51] (The organization of the initial RAMSI military component appears in Figure 1.6.) Civilians represented a considerable number of other functions and organizations in addition to DFAT: the Australian Agency for International Development (AusAID, the nation's governmental aid organization), New Zealand's International Aid and Development Agency (NZAID), treasury, finance, and oversight and coordination teams among them.[52] Altogether such a presence was insufficient to simultaneously dominate and suppress all resistance across a population of 530,000 and many islands, but its numbers were by no means negligible given that RAMSI's capabilities were concentrated where most appropriate.

---

[48] Bryant (2005a, p. 9); McDevitt (undated, 2005b).

[49] Watson (2005a, p. 21).

[50] Bryant (2005a, p. 9).

[51] Bryant (2005a, p. 11); McDevitt (2005a); Warner (2005).

[52] Bryant (2005a, p. 11). AusAID and some other civilian agencies had in fact remained on the island during the previous difficult years, as will be discussed later.

Figure 1.6
Initial RAMSI Military Component

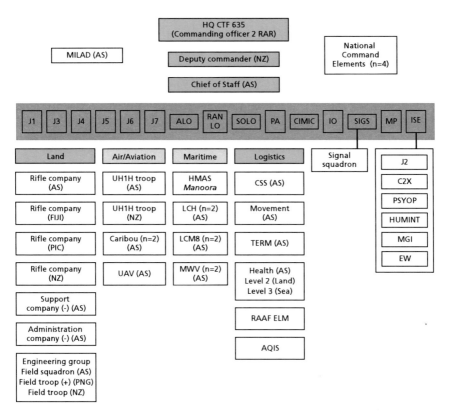

SOURCE: Provided to the author by Lieutenant Colonel John J. Frewen.
NOTES: 2RAR = 2nd Battalion, Royal Australian Regiment; ALO = air liaison officer;
AQIS = Australian Quarantine Inspection Service; AS = Australia; C2X = coalition
intelligence staff section, counterintelligence and human intelligence; Caribou = type
of transport aircraft; CIMIC = civil-military coordination; CSS = combat service support;
EW = electronic warfare; HQ = headquarters; HUMINT = human intelligence;
IO = information operations; ISE = intelligence support element; J1= personnel staff
section, joint headquarters; J2 = intelligence staff section, joint headquarters;
J3 = training and operations staff section, joint headquarters; J4 = logistics staff
section, joint headquarters; J5 = plans staff section, joint headquarters;
J6 = communications staff section, joint headquarters; J7 = engineering staff section,
joint headquarters; LCH = landing craft–heavy; LCM8 = landing craft–medium, model
8; MGI = military geographic information; MILAD = military advisor; MP = military
police; MWV = minor war vessel; NZ = New Zealand; PA = public affairs; PIC = Pacific
Islands Contingent; PSYOP = psychological operations; RAAF ELM = Royal Australian
Air Force element; RAN LO = Royal Australian Navy liaison officer; SIGS = signals;
SOLO = special operations liaison officer; TERM = terminal detachment;
UAV = unmanned aerial vehicle; UH1H = model of helicopter.
RAND *MG551-1.6*

RAMSI: Deployment and Execution

Those preparing for deployment with RAMSI had little warning, much as had been the case in Bougainville and East Timor. Australia assumed the mission lead. The senior representatives of DFAT (Nick Warner), the Australian Federal Police (AFP) (Ben McDevitt), and Australian Defence Force (Lieutenant Colonel John Frewen) had, at most, ten week's warning. The span between Frewen's initial meeting with Australia's now–Chief of Defence Force General Peter Cosgrove (the same individual who had led the nation's East Timor peacekeeping operation) and deployment was only three weeks.[53] Those at lower echelons and international members of the coalition had even less; Major Donna Boulton, Frewen's chief logistics officer, had 17 days, and only ten with the task force before it left for the Solomons.[54] Most in the Australian Army had, at best, a month's notice.[55] This extremely short lead time meant that extraordinary cooperation had to be the norm if RAMSI was to succeed, and early operational successes in fact had many heroes in addition to those who actually deployed. Their importance was magnified by the ad hoc approach to building the military component of RAMSI. As in East Timor and contingencies before that, the ADF chose to "cobble together" disparate pieces of units rather than augmenting a standing command. Boulton, responsible for providing logistical support to all RAMSI agencies and national contingents in addition to her own military component, was one of many who understood the collective nature of the operation's success. She cited the importance of "the willingness of [other ADF] agencies that said, 'What do you need? We'll catch up later.' . . . I was absolutely bewildered. . . . It was amazing. . . . If I asked somebody for something, I got it."[56]

Reflecting the lesson learned regarding the effect that the USS *Belleau Wood* had off East Timor, the HMAS *Manoora* appeared off the

---

[53] Frewen (2005b).

[54] Boulton (2005).

[55] Bryant (2005a, p. 9).

[56] Boulton (2005).

Guadalcanal coast on the morning of July 24, 2003, its arrival timed deliberately to coincide with that of the first Australian Air Force C-130 Hercules aircraft landings at Henderson Field, Honiara's airport.[57] (See Figure 1.7.) Soldiers departed the planes armed and ready to defeat any resistance, accompanied by members of the police and civilian contingents who would be their colleagues in the weeks to come. Military personnel later disembarked from the *Manoora*, crossing the same Red Beach on which U.S. marines had landed in 1942. The soldiers adapted quickly to the warm greetings of the many islanders happy to have the force arrive, holding their weapons in a nonthreatening manner and returning the waves of men, women, and children. The crowd reaction lends credence to a conclusion that the coordinated arrival of ship and aircraft and the posture of the disembarking military personnel had the desired effect of demonstrating competence rather than aggression. Other naval vessels, meanwhile, patrolled the waters off shore and between Bougainville and Guadalcanal to prevent any attempts to import or export arms.[58]

RAMSI planners envisioned an operation in three phases. The first, *commencement,* was expected to last approximately six months and was meant to restore stability by disarming the population, restoring law and order, capturing militant leaders and criminals, and strengthening the police force. Phase two, *consolidation,* beginning in January 2004 and concluding a year later, would emphasize institutional reform. The final phase, *sustainability and self-reliance,* was to start in January 2005. Its focus was the development of indigenous self-reliance and the solidification of governmental and social reforms.[59] RAMSI was funded through June 2008, but it was expected that it would continue for a much longer period, a commitment that was highlighted frequently during early public pronouncements in Australia by

---

[57] Bryant (2005a, p. 15). It is the same Henderson Field used by Allied forces during World War II.

[58] Londey (2004, p. 228).

[59] Ben McDevitt in "RAMSI Press Conference" (2004).

Figure 1.7
HMAS *Manoora* Off the Solomon Islands Coast

SOURCE: Photo by LSPH David Connolly, Royal Australian Navy. Courtesy of the
Government of Australia, Department of Defence. Used with permission.
RAND *MG551-1.7*

Prime Minister John Howard and others in the Canberra government,
as well as the leadership of RAMSI itself.[60]

RAMSI quickly established base camps on Guadalcanal Beach
and at Henderson Field. Ben McDevitt's AFP contingent led the operation at the tactical level. Determined to establish precedent immediately, Australian police moved into Honiara and conducted their first
joint patrol with the RSIP on the afternoon of arrival. Military security
patrols were present at all such events when deemed necessary, albeit
in a manner and at a distance designed not to detract from the police
operations. The patrols were a vital component in giving RAMSI the
high profile desired; images of the initial patrols were beamed by media
throughout the region. The duration between this instance of police on

---

[60] Bryant (2005a, pp. 10–12); Warner (2004a).

the streets and the last such occurrence was one measured in years in many locations.[61]

The pace of other initiatives was similarly deliberately quick, with RAMSI always seeking to control the initiative. The operations leaders announced their gun amnesty program within one week of arrival. Every such weapon was to be turned in to RAMSI representatives within a three-week period, thereafter to be destroyed in public forums. (During previous weapon turn-ins, the guns were stored, resulting in a burden for the coalition force that had to guard them and causing a situation in which factions feared that the guns would be stolen and used against them, which did in fact occur. John Frewen recalled, "We had learned from Bougainville never to have weapons turned in and take them away. The people think you are taking them and giving them to their enemies. So we cut them up in front of them. We let people come out of the crowd and cut them up. It was hugely popular."[62]) Leaders and other RAMSI members spread word of their arrival and its objectives throughout the islands by way of visits to hundreds of villages and towns and through radio and newspaper notices.[63] The Australian Army's Defence Advisor to Honiara, Lt Col Luke Foster, had assisted in preparing the population for the gun amnesty prior to RAMSI's arrival, outlining its specifications and telling of the coming force's capabilities to find hidden caches.[64] Ben McDevitt later highlighted the importance and effectiveness of Foster's efforts, noting in a speech that "the first illegal firearms had been handed in even before we arrived in anticipation of the mission and overnight stolen cars suddenly appeared in owner's yards."[65] Noncompliance—not turning in guns prior to the three-week deadline—was punishable by a heavy fine and lengthy imprisonment. An "open day" demonstration of RAMSI

---

[61] Bryant (2005a, p. 12); McDevitt (2005b).

[62] Frewen (2005b).

[63] Warner (2004a).

[64] Colonel Foster's position was similar to that of a military attaché in the U.S. armed forces.

[65] McDevitt (2005b).

capabilities during the amnesty period (on August 2, 2003) helped to motivate conformity.[66] Equipment displays and demonstrations were also conducted, the intention being to convince locals that concealing guns would be a fruitless endeavor. Over 3,700 guns were surrendered within the specified time, including 700 of military quality.[67] As noted by Lt Col Frewen, RAMSI members destroyed these in full view of the population, sometimes with bystanders invited to participate. (See Figure 1.8.) The Solomon Islands citizenry strongly backed the effort. Peter Noble thought that this was due in part to the diminished status of the militants and growing public intolerance of violence that started during the IPMT years of 2000–2002. He recalled the reaction when the Malaitan Eagle Force tried to get the 2002 IPMT amnesty end date extended. Before that time,

> [T]he MEF would say a few lines and the community would fall in line, [but the IPMT campaign against weapons in the community helped to end that]. Under the law, people with arms could be declared as criminals after the arms amnesty that was to end in May 2002. The MEF wanted to extend it to December 2002, and the community told them to get stuffed. They realized they had lost their status as freedom fighters.[68]

Additionally, military operations involving numbers equivalent to a company group (approximately 120 soldiers) frequently conducted movements on one or more islands, seeking to collect information concerning warlords, criminals, and other persons of interest; capture those targeted; intimidate militia members and others with potential intent to harm RAMSI personnel or the population; provide security; and assist in further spreading the word regarding the mission's undertaking.[69]

---

[66] Bryant (2005a, p. 16). There was a second open day conducted on August 24, 2003.

[67] Warner (2004a).

[68] Noble (2005).

[69] Bryant (2005a, p. 16).

Figure 1.8
Australian Federal Police Station Sergeant Jesse Graham and Tanaghai
Village Elder Ben Show Off Two Destroyed Surrendered Weapons

SOURCE: Photo courtesy of the Government of Australia, Department of Defence,
Operation Anode photo gallery. Used with permission.
RAND *MG551-1.8*

These carefully designed actions to control the environment bal-
anced restraint with overt retention of initiative. The rules of engagement allowed soldiers to use lethal force to defend themselves and those
they were sent to protect. There were several instances in which soldiers
and police found themselves in situations in which the use of such
force was permitted under those guidelines, yet not a round was fired
in anger, a status still true as of the time of this writing in early 2006.
This patience and demonstrated good judgment reflected excellent
training and discipline. It is also a likely consequence, at least in part,
of experience during previous deployments. Many of the participating
nations' soldiers and police had served once and sometimes twice in
East Timor, as well as elsewhere, experiences that had helped to hone

their skills in making the right decision when under pressure.[70] The same restraint translated into wise practices when supporting police arrests. Although they were granted full police powers to make arrests, the military sought to allow law enforcement personnel to conduct such actions, the better to reinforce perceptions of the RSIP as the guarantors of the population's safety. Harkening back to lessons from East Timor, military lawyer James Watson noted, "Consistent with the successful approach taken by military forces during INTERFET, strict orders were given to military personnel who might be involved in detaining civilians. If it was necessary to use force to arrest a person, the minimum force necessary was to be used, the person was to be told the reason for their arrest and where they were being taken, and a friend or relative was also to be advised of this information."[71]

There was restraint of other kinds as well. Lt Col Frewen set a strict policy that his soldiers were initially not to go into towns for any but official reasons, and while there, they were not to purchase goods from local stores. His reasoning had multiple facets. First, he sought to preclude disrupting the fragile Solomon Islands economy with a sudden influx of cash and the probable resultant inflation in prices that would harm locals strapped for currency. Second, he wanted to avoid the negative impression on island youth (approximately 50 percent of the population is under 15 years of age) and broader audiences that RAMSI soldiers drinking in local establishments could present.[72] The impact on local economies was carefully controlled even later. Initially, a vehicle with 30 soldiers was allowed to visit Honiara once a week for a period of two hours. That was then expanded to two trucks a week. The concerns included those above as well as force protection. Soldiers with the chance to make the visit enjoyed the opportunity. So did the capital's citizenry, who would follow them around as they walked the city's streets.[73]

---

[70] Bryant (2005a, p. 13).

[71] Watson (2005a, p. 28).

[72] Bryant (2005a, pp. 15–16); New Zealand's International Aid and Development Agency (2004).

[73] Boulton (2005).

With this backdrop of seeking to provide a consistent and supportive image to the Solomon Islands population, RAMSI set out to accomplish the major specific tasks inherent in the first phase of its operations. Disarming the militants was priority one, the gun amnesty and information programs as discussed previously being primary elements. A second task was obtaining the surrender of key militant leaders, Guadalcanal Liberation Front leader Harold Keke foremost in that regard. Cruelty and violence had characterized Keke's control of the densely forested mountain region and the coastline that his militia occupied, and his was the best trained of the major militia groups. Atrocities included numerous murders, among them the killing of seven Anglicans from the Melanesian Brothers order who had been taken hostage in May 2000.[74] On another occasion, Keke's men entered the village of Marassa during the early morning hours and gathered its residents. The hands of all males were bound and the entire assemblage was herded to the beach, where they were kept for two and a half days in scorching weather. Two young men, aged 15 and 19, were separated from the group, as they had earlier been observed taking pictures. Keke had determined that they must therefore be spies. Both were beaten to death. Marassa was subsequently burned to the ground, the only exception being the church, spared due to Keke's strong religious beliefs.[75]

The RAMSI principals—Warner, McDevitt, and Frewen—held three meetings with Keke during the first days after their arrival, eventually convincing him to surrender. McDevitt described the importance of the capitulation given that Harold Keke and his deputy, Ronnie Cawa, "knew every inch of the terrain" on the Weathercoast and that his militia was the most able of the factions that could have resisted RAMSI:

> They were very fit, and well drilled. . . . If we'd had to go in there, we would have suffered fairly significant casualties. . . . As it was, Harold had such psychological control over his lieutenants that

---

[74] Nick Warner (2004a).

[75] McDevitt (2005a).

we had him write letters back and tell them who we wanted to arrest. We called it arrest by appointment. They would come out of the jungle in dozens. They would stand on the beach, and we'd pick them up by helicopter, take them back to Honiara, charge them with murder, then go back for another group.[76]

Keke's surrender was a truly interagency and joint military event. After extended negotiations, initiated by Ben McDevitt with a letter to Keke prior to RAMSI's arrival and continued collectively by the Big Three (Warner, McDevitt, and Frewen) after arrival, Keke was persuaded to go offshore to the Australian navy's *Manoora*, where he was placed under arrest without resistance.[77] The ship had consistently been a centerpiece in demonstrating RAMSI's potential might, and separating Keke from his support eased execution of the formal arrest. John Frewen believed that "the commitment of the *Manoora* was one of the most important decisions in the operation. We never could have arrested Harold Keke without it."[78] The importance of the navy to RAMSI's general success was further evident in the desire of both Nick Warner and Ben McDevitt to keep the ship in theater. Such was not to be, however. The *Manoora*'s departure was the first step in downsizing the military force, a choice influenced by the fact that its crew had been returning from Iraq when rerouted to support the Solomons operation for an additional 90 days of deployment.[79]

---

[76] McDevitt (2005a).

[77] Keke and other faction leaders were tried and convicted of various crimes in the ensuing months. The official government announcement of Keke's conviction read as follows:

> Today Harold Keke, Ronnie Cawa and Francis Lela were found guilty of the murder of Father Augustine Geve in the High Court of Solomon Islands. They were found to have murdered Father Geve on a Weathercoast beach in August 2002. All three were sentenced to life in jail. The verdict also symbolises that no person in Solomon Islands is above the law. (Downer and Ellison, 2005)

[78] Frewen (2005b).

[79] Frewen (2005b).

Figure 1.9
Militia Leader Harold Keke and Australian Federal Police Officer Ben McDevitt During Negotiations

SOURCE: Photo courtesy of the Government of Australia, Department of Defence, Operation Anode photo gallery. Used with permission.
RAND MG551-1.9

Demonstrating that the GLF had not been a negligible threat, RAMSI won the formal surrender of its remaining members, including their disciplined formation in ranks and the performance of a weapons clearance drill for Lt Col Frewen's inspection of each piece. In the end, Keke's surrender and the resultant demise of his movement was due to adroit negotiation by the AFP's Ben McDevitt, patience and restraint on the part of the army, and the trust the Big Three had cultivated in their lengthy written and verbal negotiations with the GLC's leader. Frewen cited four factors when asked what was behind Keke's decision to terminate GLF resistance: (1) exhaustion after years of activity and involvement in the rampant Weathercoast violence, to include internecine struggles with the IFM; (2) Keke's desire to have his story told; (3) the GLF leader's belief that God had come to him in a dream and had sent Nick Warner to him; and (4) the intimidating strength of

RAMSI's military force.[80] There was also willingness by the Big Three to compromise on minor points in the service of the ultimate objective. Keke, for example, asked for and received guarantees that his wife would be well taken care of once he was in custody.[81] Success was ultimately the result of knowing one's adversary and orchestrating the combined capabilities of the interagency force to perfect effect.

Keke's surrender at once set a precedent and removed a major excuse for other militia's retaining arms and refusing to surrender. With Keke and his cohorts imprisoned, the most able and threatening of the militia and criminal groups was neutralized. Other leaders could no longer justify their lack of cooperation in terms of fearing attacks by the Guadalcanal Liberation Front, something they had done prior to the GLF's dissolution. Nick Warner explained the Big Three's method of dealing with the former militants, many of whom had become gangsters:

> Because of the purely criminal nature of most of their activities, it was decided that we would approach the former militants as a policing issue. . . . In these first few weeks, when we were asking militants to hand back weapons, we announced publicly that we were prepared to meet and talk to any of the militants, at any time, anywhere. Some Solomon Islanders saw this as a sign of weakness. They wanted arrests, not discussions, and were afraid that we would make compromises with those they feared the most. That was not our intention, and I explained at the time that RAMSI would not negotiate, or compromise or do any deals.[82]

Although Warner made it a policy to not compromise on substantive issues, his earlier willingness to agree to Harold Keke's request that his wife be treated well demonstrated his tactical flexibility in the service of accomplishing strategic objectives.

Warner cited a final major area of initial emphasis and success: progress in reintroducing a legitimate police force. Corruption was rife.

---

[80] Frewen (2005b, 2006).

[81] Frewen (2005b).

[82] Warner (2004a).

Police took food from the local population and were frequently intoxicated. Relatives in other branches of the government would pad officers' paychecks, and on more than one occasion, police forcibly removed funds from a Honiara bank.[83] A former chief of police was assassinated by a police sergeant in mid-2003, an action taken as a warning by the then–serving commissioner.[84] In Warner's words, the STAR force "had become something of a private army for those demanding money from the government. Many senior RSIP officers had also been promoted well beyond their capabilities."[85]

AusAID's work during the months prior to RAMSI's arrival paid significant dividends in addressing these widespread problems, as did interactions of RAMSI police and soldiers with the local population. One of AusAID's initiatives since the September 2000 signing of the Townsville Peace Agreement had been the development of a professional police force that would be dedicated to the people and free of graft. Those loyal to the concept—including local police and supporting administrative personnel—kept records of corruption that were invaluable to Ben McDevitt's investigators once RAMSI arrived.[86] The information became available once people gained confidence in RAMSI's long-term commitment to correcting the nation's problems.[87] Speaking in March 2004, Nick Warner would be able to look back and report that "since July 2003, over 50 RSIP members have been arrested and over 400 have been sacked. Both Deputy Commissioners have been arrested for fraud and abuse of office."[88] In short, the RSIP of July 2003 contained far too much chafe and little wheat, a situation RAMSI dealt with immediately and effectively.

Corruption was not limited to the police alone. It was a disease that had infected virtually every aspect of the governmental process.

---

[83] Foster (2005); Noble (2005).

[84] Foster (2005).

[85] Warner (2005).

[86] Foster (2005).

[87] McDevitt (2005a).

[88] Warner (2004a).

Ben McDevitt and others responsible for its eradication understood that dealing with it would take time. The availability of records, the willingness of people at various levels to come forward, political connections, and other factors all meant that progress would demand the same patient and calculated approach that was necessary in dealing with police shortcomings. Locals were particularly anxious for action against the "big fish" who had long taken advantage of their positions at the top tiers of national government; but building cases against these individuals was more demanding of all resources, time among them, than was the case for those at lower echelons. McDevitt conducted an operational maneuver that broke critical links in the feeding chain of depravity even as investigations continued, thereby interrupting ongoing theft and setting the conditions for long-term solutions:

> In the AFP we have an hourglass model. At the bottom are the disaffected youth who had status because they had a gun or were members of some organization like the Malaitan Eagle Force. In the middle were the facilitators, those with special skills or the tactical commanders. Some were commanders in the Malaitan Eagle Force; some were police; some were ex-police. At the top were the corrupt politicians who weren't keen on RAMSI because we were interfering with their getting money through corruption. We went after the middle group, the facilitators, because that separated the corrupt politician at the top from the bottom element and thus isolated the two.[89]

There was also a geographic element to McDevitt's law enforcement plan, one that influenced wider RAMSI operations, as it was the police who had the mission lead at the tactical level. Sounding much like the classic counterinsurgency "oil spot" approach in which forces secure and pacify an area, later moving outward from that point, RAMSI's leaders had their own strategy:

---

[89] McDevitt (2005a). Thanks to David Kilcullen for noting the operational maneuver character of McDevitt's approach (Kilcullen, 2006b).

Honiara was the capital. It was the seat of government. It was where the majority of the urban residents were. The first thing we wanted to do was win back the streets of Honiara. Then we went out to the real hot spots. . . . I think it was day 14 that we set up the first police outpost on the Weathercoast . . . and then we spread out and made sure we weren't appearing to favor any one group. . . . We used the police stations to spread messages. Some of them were police messages, but some were about other events, like sporting events. And we bought the local paper [that had] a circulation of about 3,000 just in Honiara and posted it up open behind plastic [at the police outposts]. And people would walk tens of kilometers just to read the paper, to find out what was going on. The police stations became real [hubs of social activity and sources of information].[90]

As with Cosgrove's deliberate expansion of INTERFET efforts in East Timor, such an approach recognized that RAMSI lacked sufficient personnel to simultaneously secure the entirety of the Solomon Islands. It is indeed questionable that such an approach would have been desirable even had the personnel been available. The measured advances provided time for the coalition's legitimacy to gain sway with the local population, thereby dramatically expanding the number of information sources so crucial to exorcising militia, criminal, and other undesirable elements from the ailing society. The deliberate approach also provided means for the Big Three to continually reinforce vital messages. Nick Warner and Ben McDevitt would personally lead ceremonies for the opening of police outposts, emphasizing the Solomon Islander–RAMSI character of the law enforcement effort and other elements important to the operation's continued success.[91]

As envisioned, initial successes allowed RAMSI to refocus its resources and transition to the second phase of the operation. The coalition's men and women increasingly turned toward nation-building activities. Nine months after its arrival, civilians made up a much greater portion of RAMSI, the number of military personnel

---

[90] McDevitt (2005a).

[91] McDevitt (2005a).

having been reduced from a peak of some 1,800 in the early months to 700 by March 2004. The maneuver force shrank from four infantry companies to a single, albeit large, Pacific Island company with representatives of the several participating armies.[92]

The dramatic progress during these early months did not mean that the operation was not without risks and challenges. Lt Col Frewen and many in the first RAMSI military rotation returned to home stations after approximately three and a half months, Frewen surrendering command of CTF 635 to the Australian Army's Lt Col Quentin Flowers. Lt Col John Hutcheson followed Flowers in turn, and so it continued, with military and other personnel coming to the Solomon Islands to assume responsibilities from their predecessors. Participating nations' leaders adjusted the numbers of their personnel as mission demands changed. By late 2004, over a year after RAMSI's initial entry into the operational area, the military representation had been dramatically reduced. It numbered approximately 60 personnel, a reflection of the successes in diminishing the threat from militia and gang elements.[93] During the early morning hours of December 22, 2004, Australian policeman Adam Dunning was twice struck in the back by automatic-weapon rounds while patrolling in Honiara.[94] Dunning died, RAMSI's first fatality. Reaction was swift. Although there was no evidence that the event was anything other than the action of a lone criminal, the Australians immediately dispatched a quick-reaction force of reinforced company size from the mainland, raising the military strength to over 250 within 24 hours of the incident.[95] The deployment and the reasons underlying it were pointedly broadcast to a wide audience for maximum effect. That any further violence would be dealt with severely was evident in the posture of the reinforcements; they patrolled with the RSIP while heavily armed and attired in helmets

---

[92] Warner (2004a).

[93] Hutcheson (2006).

[94] "Peacekeeper Shot Dead in Solomons" (2004).

[95] Flowers (2005); Hutcheson (2006). Flowers described the unit as a "high-readiness rifle company group" numbering approximately 200 personnel. Flowers had served as Cosgrove's head planner for operations in East Timor.

and other combat gear to emphasize the message. (See Figure 1.10.) The announcement also capitalized on the opportunity to reinforce the coalition's long-term commitment to success:

> Following the tragic death of Adam Dunning, an Australian Federal Police Protective Service Officer, . . . An infantry company out of the 2nd Royal Australian Regiment [sic; it was the 1st Royal Australian Regiment] will commence its redeployment tomorrow, 23 December. This redeployment underscores the Government's determination not to be intimidated and demonstrates its commitment to completing RAMSI's mission in Solomon Islands.[96]

The rapid deployment had the dual impact of forestalling any troublesome group's resurgent ambitions, should that have proved a threat, while also demonstrating to militias, criminals, and innocents alike that there would be no tolerating a return to the violence that plagued the country prior to RAMSI's arrival.

The possible challenge to RAMSI's maintenance of security had counterparts on the political front:

> The Solomon Islands invited us in because they [many government officials] couldn't make enough money off of corruption and graft. . . . What they wanted to do was get rid of the criminals on the streets, and then get rid of us so they could start making money again. But Australia and New Zealand would have none of it. We had too much invested. . . . The people want us to stay.[97]

The refusal to be satisfied with addressing only the Solomon Islands' immediate problems was consistent with the policies established by Australia and its RAMSI partners since Prime Minister John Howard's decision to deploy a force in response to his Solomon

---

[96] Downer (2004). Correction to unit that deployed the rapid response company thanks to Lt Col John Frewen (2006) and Australian Government, Department of Defence (2004, image JPAU24DEC04NR130).

[97] Anonymous interview.

Figure 1.10
Private Shaun Dwyer, 1st Battalion, The Royal Australian Regiment,
Patrolling Honiara with an RSIP Officer in the Aftermath of Adam
Dunning's Murder

SOURCE: Photo courtesy of the Government of Australia, Department of Defence,
Operation Anode photo gallery. Used with permission.
RAND *MG551-1.10*

Islander counterpart's request for assistance. Despite adapting to meet
evolving conditions and operational success, RAMSI's basic foundational elements were continuously maintained. The mandate agreed
to with the island nation's political leadership was clear; as noted previously, RAMSI was to "reinforce and uphold the legitimate institutions and authorities in the Solomon Islands, and to ensure respect for
the country's constitution and implementation of its laws."[98] Instituting this mandate involved the implementation of several policies that
served to guide those instituting actions, from the highest echelons in
participating nations' capitals to the men and women providing aid to
the Solomon Islands' citizens, patrolling the nation's communities, or

---

[98] Bryant (2005a, p. 9).

accomplishing the myriad other tasks upon which the mission's success relied on the islands themselves. These policies included

- unfailing dedication to a long-term commitment
- preservation of the Solomon Islands' sovereignty and laws
- firm limitations on the scope of the mandate; while RAMSI would vigorously address those elements of the nation's society that threatened the welfare of its citizens—corruption, limited education, and violence, among others—it would not otherwise impose external social or moral standards on the people
- consideration that it was always the people, and the governmental authorities who were to serve them, who were ultimately the primary vehicles of progress. RAMSI participants worked with and alongside Solomon Islanders to restore peace and stability while building the capabilities for a more secure future. Ben McDevitt was made a member of the RSIP. Other RAMSI police officers patrolled alongside Solomon Islander law enforcement personnel. Those providing expertise to government staff sections did so in conjunction with indigenous authorities. RAMSI was there to help at the request of the country's executive and legislative powers; it unceasingly maintained its status as invitees rather than assuming the role of occupier. Leaders in Canberra, Wellington, and other participating nations' capitals supported their personnel on the ground and the islands' citizens, resisting efforts by corrupt Solomon Islander politicians to oust the outsiders, politicians who had perhaps gotten more than they bargained for from their initial invitation. Ultimately, however, RAMSI maintains its presence at the discretion of the Solomon Islands' prime minister, parliament, and, ultimately, its citizens.

Patience on the ground has been accompanied by a similar fortitude at the strategic level. Mark Bonser, the Chief of Defence Force representative in Australia to whom John Frewen reported while commanding the CTF 635, recognized that success demands the orchestration of both near-term victories and a willingness to stay on what can be a very long course:

"I think we need to put success in terms of initial success and long-term success. What we were looking for initially was a secure environment in which longer-term success" could be brought about. This involved such activities as ridding the Solomon Islands of weapons and armed criminals and establishing a viable police force. The longer term, "which I think will go on for a decade or more," involves establishing infrastructure and employment so that "youth don't become cannon fodder for criminal gangs."[99]

RAMSI as a Counterinsurgency Operation

The preceding brief overview provides the context for consideration of RAMSI as a counterinsurgency (COIN) operation. The following chapters explore such a consideration, first reviewing current conceptualizations of insurgency and counterinsurgency in Chapter Two that are followed, in turn, by an analysis of the Solomon Islands operation in light of that review in Chapters Three through Six. Chapter Three views the Solomon Islands and whether the situation there qualified as an insurgency from the perspectives of those participating in the earliest phases of RAMSI. The relevance of three functions often critical to COIN success is the foundation for Chapter Four: orchestrating interagency capabilities, multinational operations, and the significance of shaping the indigenous population's perspectives of the insurgency and efforts to counter it. Chapter Five directly addresses the question of whether conditions in the Solomon Islands constituted an insurgency and whether RAMSI therefore in fact has COIN implications. The sixth and final chapter mines the three areas considered in Chapter Four for elements that also have potential application to stability undertakings—and perhaps counterinsurgency operations—both those ongoing and those yet to come.

The timing of the interviews and other research conducted in support of this effort inherently put constraints on the final product. Its focus is on the early months of an operation conceived of in terms of an ultimate span of five or more years. The analysis and conclusions

---

[99] Bonser (2005). Portions not in quotation marks are paraphrased.

are therefore limited to those that might be drawn from these first phases; there will very likely be much more of value forthcoming as RAMSI continues. That road will inevitably be characterized by both smooth sailing and rough spots. Even as the drafts of this document were in progress, political turmoil precipitated violent demonstrations that led to injuries within the RAMSI force. Yet, both the smooth and rough will provide fodder for learning and further contemplation of the thoughts and recommendations that appear in these pages.

This is not a comprehensive account of RAMSI and all its facets. Historians, political scientists, and others with relevant expertise—to include participants—will, hopefully, undertake both broader analyses and ones more specific in future years. These pages provide an overview, one that favors a security perspective and relies heavily on Australian and New Zealand perspectives. The thoughts of Solomon Islanders themselves and insights to be gained from RAMSI members representing other participating nations receive less attention than is desirable due to the opportunities for interviews and the nature of written sources available to the author. There is much to be gained in more thoroughly investigating functional areas that receive limited attention here, including areas pertaining to economic development, building political legitimacy, the installation of a professional ethic, information management, and preliminary diplomatic initiatives. All have implications for better understanding governments in turmoil, social devolution, and other challenges that are unfortunately too often shared by many countries around the world. The author offers this study with the hope that it will offer some value to efforts to achieve that better understanding.

CHAPTER TWO

Considering the Nature of Insurgency and Counterinsurgency

There has never been much doubt that the main characteristic which distinguishes campaigns of insurgency from other forms of war is that they are primarily concerned with the struggle for men's minds, since only by succeeding in such a struggle with a large enough number of people can the rule of law be undermined and constitutional institutions overthrown. Violence may play a greater or lesser part in the campaign, but it should be used very largely in support of ideas. In a conventional war the reverse is more usually the case and propaganda is normally deployed in support of armed might.

—Frank Kitson (1977)

They don't like bloody victories. . . . What they are really proud of is outwitting the enemy. . . . Their idea of quitting themselves like men is to achieve victory by means of something which only man possesses, that is, by the power of the intellect.

—Thomas More, Utopia

The Nature of Insurgency and Counterinsurgency

The U.S. Army describes stability operations as those that "promote and protect US national interests by influencing the threat, political, and information dimensions of the operational environment through a combination of peacetime developmental, cooperative activities and coercive actions in response to crisis."[1] RAMSI obviously qualifies (the United States' nation-centric character of the definition notwithstanding), and it therefore has lessons of potential value given the frequency of such actions in recent years. It is far less clear that it qualifies as a counterinsurgency undertaking, defined in U.S. doctrine as "[t]hose military, paramilitary, political, economic, psychological, and civic actions taken by a government to defeat insurgency."[2]

The next question is therefore whether the activities in the Solomon Islands constituted an insurgency, "[a]n organized movement aimed at the overthrow of a constituted government through the use of subversion and armed conflict," in the words of U.S. joint military doctrine.[3] Yet this is but one of many definitions. Others, and the discussions illuminating them, provide further insights regarding what constitutes an insurgency and what a current definition ought to include. For example, the Central Intelligence Agency's (CIA's) *Guide to the Analysis of Insurgency* defines insurgency as

> a protracted political-military activity directed toward . . . the use of irregular military forces and illegal political organizations. Insurgent activity . . . is designed to weaken government control and legitimacy while increasing insurgent control and legitimacy. The common denominator of most insurgent groups is their desire to control a particular area. This objective differentiates insurgent groups from purely terrorist organizations, whose objectives do not include the creation of an alternative government capable of controlling a given area or country.[4]

There are at least two interesting elements in this offering that contradict or expand on the joint military definition. First, in the CIA

---

[1]   Headquarters, U.S. Department of the Army (2001, p. 1-15).

[2]   Joint Chiefs of Staff (2001, p. 127). The initial draft of the joint U.S. Army Field Manual and USMC Reference Publication *Counterinsurgency* retains this definition and that for *insurgency*. (See Headquarters, U.S. Department of the Army, and Headquarters, U.S. Marine Corps, 2006, p. 1-1).

[3]   Joint Chiefs of Staff (2001, p. 262).

[4]   CIA *Guide to the Analysis of Insurgency*, quoted in Byman (2005, pp. 4–5).

wording, an insurgency does not require "the overthrow of a constituted government," but rather includes the more limited objectives of weakening government control while enhancing insurgent legitimacy and control. It is also significant that the control sought need only apply to "a particular area," one that could conceivably entail a very limited expanse, an entire country, or a region that overlaps several countries.

Current U.S. Army counterinsurgency doctrine expands on the joint services' definition, sharing the elements of political character, legitimacy, and control with the CIA wording. Insurgency "is a protracted politico-military struggle designed to weaken government control and legitimacy while increasing insurgent control. Political power is the central issue in an insurgency."[5] However, the U.S. Army's discussion emphasizes that the insurgent's focus is ultimately replacement of a standing government: "The goal of an insurgency is to mobilize human and material resources in order to form an alternative to the state. This alternative is called the counterstate."[6] This might at first seem to limit the application to efforts to overthrow a standing government. That need not be the case, however; the definition and accompanying text allow (intentionally or not) for the formation of an alternative to the state in a limited area rather than the replacement of a government nationwide. Other definitions tend to address overthrow at the national level more pointedly, envisioning insurgency as fundamentally a politically motivated movement seeking to replace the existent government throughout its jurisdiction. The British Army's definition shares exact wording with its American joint counterpart, but adds recognition that the objectives of an insurgency vary. This seems to imply that replacement of a government can be but a means to an end rather than an end in itself:

---

[5]   Headquarters, U.S. Department of the Army (2004, p. 1-1). As noted in footnote 2, however, the new draft counterinsurgency doctrine for both the U.S. Army and USMC reverts to the joint definition. (See Headquarters, U.S. Department of the Army, and Headquarters, U.S. Marine Corps, 2006, p. 1-1).

[6]   Headquarters, U.S. Department of the Army (2004, p. 1-1).

An insurgency is defined as an organized movement aimed at the overthrow of a constituted government through the use of subversion and armed conflict. It is an armed political struggle, the goals of which may be diverse.[7]

Further discussion accompanying the presentation of this definition muddies the waters further: "Campaigns of national resistance differ from insurgencies in that they aim to liberate a country from government by an invader, or overthrow a government imposed by an invader."[8] The nuance at first seems a legitimate one, especially given that the authors then cite the example of the French Resistance fighting the Germans during World War II. Yet what constitutes "national resistance" is often a matter of perception. Assuming the insurgents' (or national resistors') view, one could conceivably argue that no insurgency exists in early 21st-century Iraq or Afghanistan, and that none did in mid–20th-century Vietnam or reoccupied Malaya. The delineation therefore seems more troublesome than valuable. That said, it does illuminate the difficulty in sharply bounding such contingencies. Definitions might be clearly worded, but those applying them in the field will be wise to accept blurred boundaries and overlap with other efforts to categorize or provide solutions to the challenges at hand. This is all for the better—many are the disciplines that offer value in addressing insurgencies.

Most definitions of insurgency also comment on the means employed by the perpetrators. Those above provide "subversion," "armed conflict," "irregular military forces," and "illegal political organizations" in this regard. These additional definitional elements help to distinguish insurgencies from generally accepted or more familiar ways of influencing governments. Insurgencies are generally considered illegal in the sense that the approach taken does not fall within the bounds of constitutional or other officially sanctioned procedures of governmental succession. The tactics employed by a political party or other interest group seeking to put its candidates in office do not

---

[7] British Army, Directorate General, Development and Doctrine (2005, p. 17).

[8] British Army, Directorate General, Development and Doctrine (2005, p. 17).

qualify as an insurgency if they fall within the limits of commonly acceptable behavior for replacing one ruling authority with another. Similarly, while a single extreme act (such as murder) taken to remove serving leaders might mark an act in support of an insurgency, such an isolated incident lacks the sustained duration that characterizes these undertakings. A terrorist action might be a component of an insurgent group's campaign; a single terrorist strike does not itself comprise an insurgency. Thomas Mockaitis addresses some of the means and the motivations behind their use as he expands beyond envisioning an insurgency as only a politico-military undertaking:

> The insurgent seeks to gain control of a country from within and to reshape it in the image of some ideology. This aspect of insurgency is what Michael Elliot-Bateman calls 'the fourth dimension in warfare,' the social/psychological dimension.
>
> Insurgency, then, is a hybrid form of conflict that combines subversion, guerrilla warfare, and terrorism. It is an internal struggle in which a disaffected group seeks to gain control of a nation.[9]

Zachary Abuza similarly emphasizes the other-than-territorial nature of insurgencies, lending recognition to both the psychological and social domains addressed by Mockaitis. Investigating the Muslim insurgency in early 21st-century Thailand, Abuza concludes,

> There is also a misunderstanding about the nature of the insurgency. This is not an insurgency about physical space, but an insurgency about mental space. Moreover, it is an intra-Muslim conflict. Since March 2005, militants have killed more of their co-religionists than they have Buddhists. Put simply, the militants are ideologically and religiously motivated; they are trying to impose a very austere and intolerant form of Islam on their society and they countenance no opposition to this.[10]

---

[9] Mockaitis (1990, p. 3).

[10] Abuza (2006, p. 6). David Kilcullen notes that other analysts believe that "insurgents in the three southern provinces are primarily motivated by ethnic Malay separatist aspirations,"

It seems wise to investigate these definitions and perspectives more thoroughly in light of recent and ongoing stability operations of various types. Both the character of some movements and the participants' objectives seem somewhat at odds with what the definitions imply we should expect. The implications for the men and women conducting counterinsurgency operations are considerable. Are the lessons of previous counterinsurgencies to be discounted if the threat seeks only to undermine (rather than overthrow) the constituted government, or if its goal is only to wrest control of a limited geographical area away from that body rather than topple it completely? Should we forego the wisdom of past COIN operation leaders because there exists no constituted government to replace, as one might argue was the case in 1992 Somalia or 1999 East Timor? On the other hand, do we need to cast aside the benefits of employing an insurgent approach if the entity in control of the land and its people is a criminal enterprise or other nonstate actor not qualifying as a "constituted government" in the traditional sense? It seems that the concepts underlying the standing definitions of insurgency (and counterinsurgency, by extension) are too constrained by previous perceptions of the two. If the ends are similar—a government overthrown, replaced in a portion of its territory, rendered essentially nonexistent via actions political or otherwise, or whose legitimacy is undermined—it seems logical to expand the doctrine to account for insurgency's evolutions undergone since the end of the struggles in Malaya, the Vietnam War, and those conflicts that underpin the now-inadequate definitions. Similarly, in applying whatever definitions ultimately seem most appropriate, those undertaking counterinsurgency or insurgency operations need to draw selectively on the lessons of the past, employing them as sources of illumination rather than as outright solutions. Such concepts as the oil spot approach to securing areas and controlling physical spaces will have application, but too often theorists and historians alike view past insurgencies in terms of terrain dominated and walls constructed to limit access. The realm of the insurgent and counterinsurgent includes

---

but that insurgent leaders employ religion in the interest of gaining internal and external support (Kilcullen, 2006b).

the three dimensions of space. Yet even more important are the environmental features of time, perception, expectation, rumor, religion, societal bonds, social obligations, and interests and motivations. Physical space is the medium through which the insurgent moves bodily; control of that space may not be essential to an insurgency's ultimate objectives.

The threat to the government of the Solomon Islands in 2003, and more importantly to its citizens, was little similar to the historical precedents most students of conflict study. But then the struggle in 2006 Afghanistan and that in Iraq are likewise in many ways dissimilar to those earlier struggles. Certainly the ousted Taliban would like to regain control of what was formerly its Central Asian domain, but its comeback thus far compares poorly with the well-organized and frequently highly disciplined fighters who characterized the Vietcong. Taliban motivations are arguably suspect; one might question whether the desired end is resumption of power or simply the ousting of coalition forces that would permit a return to the feudal structure so long characteristic of Afghanistan, one that might find the former regime in control of only a fraction of the country. The ultimate objectives of "insurgents" in Iraq are likewise difficult to fathom, perhaps because that label has been applied to so many and so varied a collection of entities. There certainly appear to be groups seeking to replace the current Iraqi government with another, though whether that is to be a fundamentalist, more tolerant religious, or secular authority is indeterminate behind the propaganda and turmoil that characterizes Iraq at present. Other groups claiming to be or simply granted the label *insurgent* are nothing more than criminal gangs interested in taking advantage of current breakdowns in the rule of law for personal profit. A third group seems focused on the removal of coalition military representatives; it appears quite possible that they have few plans and little concern about who governs thereafter. Some factions are led and joined by foreigners. Few, if any, have an intention of supporting the assumption of Iraq's sovereignty by their native country or by another. What occupation there is with future governance includes notions of Iraq becoming part of a universal religious state. And this list is by no means exhaustive. There is a notable absence of a single, dominant insurgent movement oriented toward overthrowing Baghdad's current administration. There may be many insurgents; there is at best a fragmented, even incoherent, insurgency if one accepts the standing definitions.

Inadequacies in standing definitions should surprise no one. The nature of insurgency changes over time. War and other forms of international political intercourse likewise evolve constantly. Failure to adapt to changing conditions relegates stagnant conceptualizations, methods, and those who employ them to "the dustbin of history." The World War I insurgency of T. E. Lawrence (a.k.a. Lawrence of Arabia) and his Arab warriors was militarily very loosely structured and reliant on an ephemeral political foundation. Later efforts led by Mao Tse Tung in China and Ho Chi Minh in Vietnam demonstrated a dramatic maturation in force application and political sophistication despite the passage of only several decades.[11] We should no more expect insurgents 30 to 50 years after them to follow precisely in their footsteps than anyone reasonably could have expected them to emulate Lawrence in the years marking an equal time span after him. Yet today's definitions of *insurgency* by and large imply that we should do exactly that.

While they may suffer deficiencies, current definitions are generally well considered in the sense that they inherently account for the complexity of insurgencies. No one factor or set of factors—means, motivations, or ends sought—can alone represent what constitutes an insurgency. Focusing only on the means employed would be akin to being enamored with a process rather than the objective. Motivations are important but secondary in importance to the ultimate end sought. True, most insurgencies at least attempt to drape their apparent ambitions in the legitimacy of a political cause. Any cloak of political authenticity has long since fallen from the shoulders of the criminal Fuerzas Armadas Revolucionarias de Colombia (FARC). Similarly, somewhere over the years the Irish Republican Army (IRA) (or at least some of its splinter groups) came to possess illicit motivations driven more by self-interest than its formerly espoused political agendas. In the case of the FARC, the criminal enterprise is the de facto sovereign power in a considerable part of Colombia. Its actions undermine the legitimacy of the

---

[11] Beckett and Pimlott (1985, p. 5).

national government and deprive citizens of fundamental rights despite the criminal rather than political character of its motives.

It would therefore seem that definitions of insurgency and counterinsurgency that require political motivation and the complete overthrow of a standing government are unable to account for the present reality. Insurgent and counterinsurgent approaches alike need not rely on sincere or even false political foundations. The end sought need not be the complete overthrow of a government. Simply undermining and leaving an administration in place may serve the insurgents' purposes better given the international community's hesitation to impinge on the sovereignty of a nation state except in extremis. The insurgent may therefore seek only to take control of a portion of a country, leaving the government in place elsewhere. There are nonetheless several factors that appear to be common to both historical and current insurgent efforts.[12] First, the primary entity threatened is a constituted government (though the people almost inevitably suffer as well). Second, the ways and means employed to threaten the government must, in common with generally accepted definitions or practice, be illegal; otherwise, even legitimate intercourse such as that represented by opposing political parties would constitute insurgency.[13] The specific means are also important. While another state could replace an existing government by simply assassinating key members and imposing new rulers, the overthrow would not constitute what is understood to be insurgent action. Mao's use of the term *protracted warfare* is revealing. Insurgencies take time; they eat away at a government's legitimacy and power rather than eliminating it with a single or very limited number of conclusive blows. It is an attritional rather than an immediately decisive process. Third, force—applied or merely threatened—plays a role. A ruler's ouster through political trickery and shifting alliances alone, no matter how long the planning might have been ongoing, lacks the

---

[12] This does not imply that current insurgencies have entirely replaced those of the types fitting the stated definitions, but rather that it is inappropriate to believe that contingencies falling within the bounds of these older definitions account for the full range of insurgency profiles.

[13] The caveats *generally accepted* and *or practice* are necessary as such political processes might be illegal under some regimes.

overt struggle and, at least, the threat of violence that are inherent in insurgencies. Given these constraints, the following serves as the definition of *insurgency* underlying the remainder of this study:

> *Insurgency*: an organized movement seeking to replace or undermine all or part of the sovereignty of one or more constituted governments through the protracted use of subversion and armed conflict.[14]

As for counterinsurgency, the draft U.S. Army and USMC manual rightfully concludes that "one of the key paradoxes of insurgency and counterinsurgency [is that] they are distinctly different forms of warfare."[15] The two are by no means exact or even mirror images of each other. That does not mean that the purpose of a counterinsurgency is not in direct opposition to that of the insurgents, however. The means brought to bear and the ways they are employed will likely be wide-ranging and varied, but the ultimate purpose is nonetheless straightforward, which makes the definition equally so:

> *Counterinsurgency*: an organized effort to preclude or defeat an insurgency.

The seeming redundancy of "preclude or defeat" serves a purpose. As has long been accepted, the best time to defeat an insurgency is in its earliest stage, a point at which it may yet be unrecognized—or unrecognizable—as such an entity.

---

[14] The author thanks David Kilcullen for suggesting that the definition apply to "one or more" versus exclusively a single government (Kilcullen, 2006b).

[15] Headquarters, U.S. Department of the Army, and Headquarters, U.S. Marine Corps (2006, p. 1-1).

CHAPTER THREE

July 2003 Solomon Islands as an Insurgency: Participant Perspectives

It is clear that the leaders of the nations providing men and women to RAMSI considered the undertaking one of assisting a government and people in need. From the perspective of AusAID, for example, "The purpose of RAMSI, a regional assistance mission involving security and civil policing elements, is to restore physical and economic stability and the basic functioning of government to Solomon Islands."[1]

RAMSI participants and those in the participants' capitals are quick to remind us that the operation's ultimate success has yet to be determined, but it is evident that the initial years of that undertaking have done much to meet these goals. They did not view the threat as an insurgent one as they undertook their several missions, and their responses differed widely when they were later asked to consider whether insurgency was among the threats to the island nation in July 2003. The respondents fall into three general categories:

- those who deny that any such threat existed or could have developed given the situation of July 2003
- those who believe that such a threat did exist or would have developed
- those who believe that an insurgency might have developed over time.

---

[1] Australian Agency for International Development (2006b).

A Solomon Islands Insurgency? No

The Australian Federal Police's Ben McDevitt concludes that no insurgency could have existed, at least not in the traditional sense of a movement to overthrow the standing government. The situation had devolved into one in which there was virtually no government to overthrow:

> There was no provision of services. . . . The politicians were aligning themselves with criminal gangs. . . . No effective opposition. . . . What there was is a group of individuals who would buy votes. . . . There was no effective government that you would mount an insurgency against. There were just these groups that were fighting over land, over money. It wasn't as cohesive as I would imagine an insurgency to be, to destabilize a government, I think the government was trying to do it to itself. . . . I don't think any of them had a long-term strategy; everybody was living day-to-day for everything they could get for themselves.[2]

A Solomon Islands Insurgency? Yes

Lieutenant Colonel John Frewen, the commander of the initial RAMSI military contingent, took a slightly different tack by applying a reevaluation of what constitutes an insurgency to the July 2003 situation in the Solomon Islands. Frewen had "just recently reviewed our new counterinsurgency doctrine, and it was put to me that there is a new type of insurgency: criminal insurgency."[3] His reasoning, not dissimilar to that outlined in the previous chapter, expands on more "traditional" or Cold War definitions of insurgency to recognize that other than political motivations can underlie insurgent intentions. Presumably then, those intentions can encompass outcomes other than complete overthrow of a standing government. In this context, it seems that there is the prospect that an insurgency did threaten, or was threaten-

---

[2] McDevitt (2005a).

[3] Frewen (2005b). The Australian Army's counterinsurgency doctrine was not available for inclusion in this study.

ing, the government and people of the Solomon Islands as RAMSI arrived in July 2003.

A Solomon Islands Insurgency? Perhaps

New Zealand Major Vern Bennett, second-in-command of the first RAMSI military rotation, felt that although the Solomon Islands government had lost its ability to provide basic services by July 2003, it suffered no threat from an insurgency akin to that presented by the Vietcong in Vietnam or those resisting the government in post–World War II Malaya. Yet, criminal elements did endanger the viability of the standing government and were undeniably undermining its legitimacy. In Bennett's mind, "the potential was there" with respect to an insurgency, but the timely arrival of RAMSI and the manner with which it firmly but peacefully asserted itself had "a very stabilizing effect," one that interrupted the downward spiral toward possible fragmentation, government dissolution, overthrow, or anarchy.[4] Any latent insurgency was blocked by the effectiveness of the multinational and interagency operations conducted in the service of restoring peace and order to the islands.

Lt Col Luke Foster was of a similar mind. Beyond the bounds of Honiara, the police had no control over matters. As noted previously, some parts were dominated by leaders such as Harold Keke. These individuals were virtually autonomous in their areas of influence, free of any need to answer to the central government. They had created effectively stateless enclaves within Solomon Islands territory. However, Lt Col Foster did not feel he could accurately judge whether the criminal and militia elements that controlled those outlying areas had the desire or capability to replace the standing government.[5] He felt there was possibly the potential for development of an insurgency given the conditions immediately before RAMSI's arrival, but, like Bennett,

---

[4]   Bennett (2005a).

[5]   Foster (2005).

Foster believed that any such development was rendered moot by the arrival of the soldiers and other personnel in July 2003.

Contemplating the situation before the arrival, New Zealand's Peter Noble was "not sure it is an insurgency as you and I would understand it." While there were various groups "sucking the blood out of the state," the behavior of the leaders and members of some military groups was more "criminal or psychopathic" in character than oriented toward objectives that would fit a traditional insurgency.[6]

The Australian Defence Force's legal advisor, James Watson, cautioned against drawing conclusions based on the actions of groups rather than considering the motivations behind those actions. While political turmoil had previously led to the overthrow of national leadership, and Harold Keke was "effectively controlling Guadalcanal . . . that doesn't mean you have an insurgency problem." As mentioned previously, Watson believed that the crucial date in forestalling any possible insurgency was not that of RAMSI's arrival, but rather the signing of the IPMT treaty months before. In his mind, "That's the point at which you are moving out of the insurgency situation into the criminal situation. . . . Even though the engagement [the commitment of the IPMT force] wasn't successful, [the situation was being dealt with] at the police and political level."[7] For Watson, then, the roots of insurgency were there, at least potentially, but it was the demonstration of the international community's resolve in imposing the rule of law and restoring order that made evident the futility of pursuing insurgent objectives.

It will be recalled that Nick Warner led RAMSI at its outset as Australia's senior Department of Foreign Affairs and Trade representative. Warner believed that RAMSI

> wasn't counterinsurgency because there wasn't an insurgency. . . .
> They liked to dress themselves up as insurgents. . . . If we hadn't
> been successful in the way we picked them up, then there might
> have been something like an insurgency given the arms they had

---

[6]   Noble (2005).

[7]   Watson (2005b).

and the terrain held, [but] I don't think so with the Malaitans. . . . Once the Malaitans went back to Malaita, it devolved into criminal activity. . . . I don't see that they were becoming an insurgency [although they were well armed and had an organization]. Harold is different. He was purporting to support Guadie rights. And he was certainly holding his group together. With violence and terror, he was maintaining support in the area he controlled, but it's [giving it too much legitimacy] to call it an insurgency. It could have evolved into one, but only Harold and not the Malaitans, and there were other groups that wanted to be considered insurgents but were nothing more than thugs.[8]

A Solomon Islands Insurgency from the Perspective of RAMSI Participants? Concluding Thoughts

While senior RAMSI authorities disagree on whether an insurgency did or could have threatened the stability of the Solomon Islands, there is general agreement that the country's government and people were threatened. It also seems apparent that no mature movement to replace the national government with an alternative existed at the time of RAMSI's arrival. The Australian Army's Lt Col John Hutcheson argues that the intentions of at least some of the militia, gang, or other criminal groups "focused on creating the conditions to allow them the freedom of action to continue to control the populace to achieve their desired [criminal] ends rather than [replace] the legitimate government. This action fits with J.J. [Frewen's] comments on a 'criminal insurgency,'" and is akin to the discussion regarding the FARC earlier in this chapter, albeit on a different scale in light of the comparative immaturity of the criminal organizations in the Solomon Islands.

It is at once interesting and unsurprising that none of those interviewed had previously considered RAMSI a capability sent to interdict an insurgency. There was little evidence to inspire such a consideration given the definitions of insurgency in effect at the time. Contemplating whether an insurgency existed requires considerable analysis even given

---

[8]   Warner (2005b).

the alternative definition proposed in Chapter Two. This is evaluated further in Chapter Five. For now, suffice it to conclude that the well-orchestrated actions taken by the men and women supporting RAMSI served to restore a population's faith in their future. They initiated a process of relegitimizing a government while helping it to rebuild the capabilities essential for serving its people effectively. Political scientists, historians, members of the media, and amateur commentators alike are prone to labeling political crises with a single moniker: failed nation-state, insurgency, civil war, or one of many others. Reality is rarely so kind to those on whom the responsibility falls to address such calamities. Far more likely are situations that possess elements of numerous challenges, elements that change in proportion and influence over time. Fortunately, there are practices that enhance the chances of success regardless of the nature—or natures—of those myriad challenges.

CHAPTER FOUR

Successful COIN: Three Crucial Conditions

We now have a great deal of experience in working with other militaries in the region, and other police forces, and that is really paying off in Afghanistan and Iraq. Even though it was a very low-intensity operation, the experience of working with others has really paid off.

—Lieutenant Colonel Quentin Flowers, Commander, CTF 635,
speaking of the RAMSI experience (2005)

I characterize the Solomon Islands as a model for other contingencies, not a template, as every deployment is so different from others.

—Major Vern Bennett, New Zealand Army (2005a)

Every stability operation, each insurgency, is unique, meaning that the undertakings to meet their challenges are likewise. Among the many factors that influence success or failure are three particularly notable conditions. An inability to attain these conditions conversely characterizes operational failures. Effectively orchestrating interagency capabilities, capitalizing on multinational resources, and gaining the moral and operational high ground—the three elements in question— themselves require proficiency in a number of areas. The nature of these elements, how RAMSI established them in the service of restoring stability and security in the Solomon Islands, and consideration of selected critical subcomponents follow.

Orchestrating Interagency Capabilities: The "All of Government" Approach

> Two . . . things that worked: Having all the leadership staff together in one spot is vitally important. We did that. And secondly, what my experience with this sort of thing on the fringes of peacekeeping—Namibia, Cambodia, Bougainville, and a bit of East Timor—[told me:] There are vast differences in the way the special representatives handled it. . . . In Namibia, [it was essentially] said, "This is the plan and we're not going to take any gruff." In Cambodia, we waffled and gave a little here and there . . . and it worked to [an extent]. . . . [In the Solomon Islands] we weren't going to compromise on the key objectives. To my mind, that was another key ingredient why the operation worked. We had a clear mandate, and we didn't waver. Everybody, to include the Solomon Islanders, knew what we were there for.
> —*Nick Warner, Special Coordinator, RAMSI (2005)*

New Zealand's Peter Noble emphasized the importance of that mandate, one that simultaneously focused RAMSI efforts on selected areas crucial to mission success and—very importantly—also restricted its charter. Noble's comments highlight the critical point that the operation could not and did not seek to impinge on many critical governmental and social responsibilities. It instead limited its efforts to five areas:

> The real engine of RAMSI is its mandate: security, rule of law, government control of finances, functional government (especially bureaucracy), and economic reform. These are immensely appropriate and they have stood up well. . . . In the battle for legitimacy and public opinion, the mandate enabled RAMSI to avoid becoming involved in Solomons' issues, such as land issues, political reform, etc, that are best the preserve of Solomon Islanders themselves.[1]

---

[1]   Noble (2006).

RAMSI's signature characteristic might well be the extent to which the military, police, aid organizations, and foreign affairs organizations cooperated in addressing what they agreed to accomplish and constraining themselves to those areas. There were adaptations, differing perceptions, and necessary adjustments to be sure—NZAID and others are currently addressing the critical educational issues confronting Solomon Islanders, for example, an area not mentioned by Noble—but the perseverance of the Big Three in maintaining consistency even during changes of course and not allowing bureaucratic interests to override the operation's objectives set an example for participants at every echelon. To their credit, the senior representatives of the Australian Army, the Australian Federal Police, and DFAT actively sought to work out any disagreements between themselves and with their multinational and interagency partners, thereby presenting a united front to Canberra in communications sent home.[2]

This state of affairs was the result of hard work, cooperation, and a willingness to compromise. Part of that hard work was an ongoing effort by RAMSI participants to educate each other about their respective organizations. Ben McDevitt, for example, was taken aback during his participation in a military planning exercise held in the weeks before deployment. He found that the military players constructed their plan with no civilian police representation, believing that military police personnel could speak for the AFP and other nations' law enforcement organizations. In so doing, they overlooked not only critical requirements, but similarly failed to draw on colleagues' strengths of which they were unaware. For example, McDevitt noted that the army's planners didn't "realize that the bread and butter of civilian police is negotiation."[3] The importance of this potential oversight is difficult to overstate given McDevitt's crucial role in the later arrest of Harold Keke. The military, on the other hand, found that civil police planning at times proceeded without what could have

---

[2] AusAID was the fourth major organization from that country. It had representatives in the country before the arrival of RAMSI; its vital contributions are discussed later in this study.

[3] McDevitt (2005a).

been beneficial military involvement.[4] As any who have been involved in crisis planning will attest, the pressures to expedite the process by keeping the number involved to the minimum essential are considerable. Yet COIN and other stability operations demand greater participation by a broader range of organizations than is generally the case in "traditional" wartime combat; planners and leaders need to ensure that they budget the time and develop the procedures so that subordinates do not overlook these critical participants. RAMSI included many groups that were less familiar with each other's capabilities than was desirable. All now realize that this is an area in need of improvement. That the various agencies later cooperated so well, both internally and externally, is nevertheless commendable given the mere days available for preparation. John Frewen recalled with notable understatement that his soldiers' training with the police prior to deployment consisted of but six hours; his own headquarters had only an additional six hours of internal collective training beyond that, periods "obviously too short to be comprehensive."[5]

The representatives of the four principal functional areas (military, police, foreign affairs, and aid) pushed hard to gain the maximum advantage from the few interagency sessions the short predeployment period allowed. In addition to the above-noted planning event, an interagency rehearsal proved to be "absolute gold dust" in working out participant expectations and dealing with potential misunderstandings before they handicapped operations on the ground.[6] The rehearsal involved representatives from the four principal organizations, the senior representatives of which sat at a head table. Colonel (later Brigadier) Paul Symon, Nick Warner's military advisor, assumed the role of facilitator, walking participants "through the first minutes, days, and months" of the pending operations. Those present frequently raised their hands to interrupt and communicate that their vision of the

---

[4] Frewen (2005b).

[5] Frewen (2005b).

[6] Frewen (2005b).

undertaking was different from what others expected.[7] The group then worked to resolve such differences in understanding. While this session was vital, it was insufficient to close all the gaps in the mutual understanding of capabilities. John Frewen believed that "we should have had a session where DFAT, the military, and the police got together and said what they do, how they operate, and what [their] capabilities are—information sessions for other agencies."[8]

The seemingly mundane issue of lacking a common location from which to coordinate deployment from Australia also threatened to impede the rapid integration of RAMSI participants. Ben McDevitt recognized the shortfall and made the AFP's Majura facility on the outskirts of Canberra available as an "impromptu interagency headquarters," a "one-stop shop" for the many preparing for action.[9] The facility proved valuable in precluding the unnecessary travel and other sources of coordination delays that otherwise would have been unavoidable.

Such dedication to overcoming obstacles diminished the impact of what could have been crippling hindrances. During preparation for deployment, RAMSI's senior logistics officer, Major Donna Boulton, found the planning and rehearsal sessions invaluable despite their limited number and duration. She was also extremely impressed with the extent to which military staff planners ensured that the necessary logistical representatives participated.[10] This appreciation of logistical planning's importance *within* the many agencies was unfortunately not as effectively replicated *between* them. While the understanding of logistical needs within the military was by and large commonly accepted, for example, that between the army and police ran into those organizations' very different expectations, a problem given that the army had the responsibility to support all RAMSI participants. Boulton's duties included maintenance and fueling of vehicles, tasks that in the army are to a considerable extent the responsibility of those whose job

---

[7] Frewen (2005b).

[8] Frewen (2005b).

[9] Bryant (2006).

[10] Boulton (2005).

it is to operate them. Police, on the other hand, depend on centralized maintenance facilities to a great extent. The difference in points of view became starkly—and in retrospect humorously—evident one evening during the first RAMSI deployment. Boulton recalled,

> There was a case with the AFP and a four-wheel-drive vehicle. They didn't know to engage the hubs. They got it stuck and then called us to fix it. The request was a "priority one. The flight was a one-hour flight out and one hour back. . . . If it's one of my guys, I say, 'Hey, hoof it out, buddy.' . . . They're not trained to think like that." When their car breaks down at home, they just call someone to come fix it.[11]

Similarly, some AFP personnel desired to have the vehicle refueling facility open 24 hours a day. Boulton suggested that the additional personnel burden such hours would place on the mission was unnecessary given that vehicles were only being refueled once every eight days on average.[12]

Ben McDevitt's surprise at the military police not asking their civilian counterparts to participate in plan development was likely explained more by a mistaken belief that "police planning is police planning" regardless of whether it is military or civil, rather than a neglect of AFP concerns. The Royal Australian Corps of Military Police (RACMP) planners perhaps assumed that they could adequately represent AFP needs and capabilities. Such assumptions result from a lack of familiarity. Rear Admiral Mark Bonser was responsible for oversight of Australia's military RAMSI commitment from his location in Sydney. He recalled, "Police and military are completely different in the way they approach their business. Police approach it on a case-by-case basis . . . until they have enough to act on. Military [build their capabilities] so that they can survive in a conflict environment" that might confront them with a broad range of challenges, all of which

---

[11] Boulton (2005). The passages not in quotation marks are paraphrased.

[12] Boulton (2005).

they need to be prepared for.[13] The result was that "it took us quite a while to blend together," a condition amplified by the extremely short predeployment notice and limited interagency contacts in the months and years before RAMSI.[14] Fortunately for all involved—and for the success of the operation—the environment on arrival in the Solomon Islands was largely a permissive one. Such lessons are far more costly to learn under fire.

Although disagreements and misunderstandings occasionally caused frustrations, the shared mindset that they would not be allowed to interfere with mission accomplishment meant that their impact rarely reached a critical point. Patience and humor both played a role in this regard. Donna Boulton found that support expectations by those in other branches of the service or other nations' militaries differed from those of Australian Army soldiers. As is often the case during field operations in developing nations, potable water was a limited commodity on the Solomon Islands and rationing was necessary. Not all members of RAMSI had the same conception of what conservation entailed. Educating everyone with respect to the common standard, and a bit of joking, went a long way toward resolving issues in Boulton's view:

> In the military, when it comes to a shower, we know to "Get in. Turn it on. Get wet. Turn it off." . . . AFP get in, turn it on, have a shave, wash their hair. . . . "What do you mean I can't wash my hair every day?" . . . Kiwi [New Zealand] helicopter pilots: "What do you mean I can't wash my clothes in the washing machine every other day? . . . What do you mean I can't have a shower every day?" Hey, mate, I don't care if you're pilots or not. . . . You have New Zealand rotary-wing pilots and you have Australian rotary-wing pilots. We don't treat our pilots nicely. In New Zealand they do. I treated them like we treat ours . . . so I used to send them flowers once a week.[15]

---

[13] Bonser (2005).

[14] Weller (2005).

[15] Boulton (2005). While New Zealand helicopter pilots are members of the country's air force, Australian rotary-wing crews are part of the Australian Army.

The differences in approach extended beyond logistics. The army found that the more deliberate deployment timings of the police somewhat delayed the initiation of full-capacity operations after arrival on the islands. Both cultural differences and expectations regarding the length of deployment tours influenced the two organizations' approaches. Major Charles Weller, John Frewen's chief of staff, recognized that dissimilar perspectives underlay misunderstandings; likewise, the short predeployment period prevented the military and police from better understanding each other. Weller recalled that for the police, "there wasn't that fusing and then disseminating across the board. . . . It took them two to two and a half months to get their full strength on board," and in the meantime they were oriented on building up their capability rather than full-scale operations, unlike the army. "They were looking very much at the long term: six, seven, eight years from the very outset. We were looking at sixty to ninety days" based on guidance given in Australia.[16] (Police tours during RAMSI were a year in duration, as was Nick Warner's deployment. Military units rotated approximately every four months. The leadership continuity inherent in Ben McDevitt and Nick Warner's yearlong tours, a period during which the military component's senior members rotated several times, was likely a vital element in sustaining unity of message and otherwise helping RAMSI to maintain continuity of policy and influence.) The differences in deployment time are readily explained by differences in organization as well. Militaries frequently put units in quick-reaction or short-notice deployment status; the organization fulfilling that role at a given time is constantly prepared to assemble, load, and set out with limited notice. Few organizations outside of the military maintain a unit in such a state, and certainly not for international contingencies. Both this difference in approach, and the fact that the initial group of RAMSI police would be staying three to four times longer than their military counterparts, helps to explain law enforcement's greater deployment times.

Group Captain Shaun Clarke was New Zealand's senior military representative during the first RAMSI rotation. He noted that a lack

---

[16] Weller (2005).

of interagency familiarity also has potentially significant implications at the lowest tactical levels: "The police wanted to walk up to a house and say, 'Hello, Mrs. Manch. We're here to inspect your house. May we come in?' And we [the military] said, 'You're going to get killed that way.'"[17] Clarke's observation highlights a problem that affects both international and domestic contingencies involving military and police cooperation. Major General James Delk, commanding the California Army National Guard Division assisting local authorities during the 1992 riots in Los Angeles, emphasized the importance of knowing how one's counterparts operate, and the language they use to control those operations:

> Communications and language. This is very important. . . . A platoon to many cops is 60 soldiers, while there may be only 20 or less in a tank platoon. But there are other communications differences. The worst incident occurred in Compton. In Compton, which was marine territory, two Compton police officers took a squad of marines with them and headed out to a domestic dispute. The cops walked up to the door, knocked, and the next thing you know someone fired birdshot through the door. One policeman was hit, but not hurt. His partner grabbed him and as he pulled him back he hollered to the marines[,] "Cover me!" Now to a cop, that was a very simple command. That means aim your rifle and use it if necessary. To a marine, and there were some well-trained young patriots in that squad, it meant something entirely different. They instantly opened up. A mom, a dad, and three children occupied that house. I later asked the Compton police department to count the bullet holes for me because there was a rumor going around there were 50 or so rounds fired. The police told me there were over 200 bullet holes. In some cases you couldn't tell how many bullets had gone through. They didn't hit anyone, but the point is, those great young marines did exactly what they're trained to do, but not what the police thought they requested. You need to understand the differences in language.[18]

---

[17] Clarke (2005).

[18] Delk (2000, pp. 135–136).

Overcoming such differences requires a basic understanding of fellow agencies and the challenges they confront. The following two sections provide background information on the two major components of RAMSI with which both leaders and the rank and file of the military found themselves working: the police and aid agencies.

Law Enforcement Support to RAMSI

The police force that led the RAMSI law enforcement effort and was in charge of tactical operations was created in 1979 to give Australia a truly federal law enforcement capability, one responsible for investigating crimes against the nation, coordinating counterterrorism efforts, policing airports and the Australia Capital Territory (Canberra and its immediate surrounds), and escorting selected VIPs. (See Figure 4.1.) It was also tasked with assisting other Commonwealth of Australia investigative bodies, a responsibility complemented by the 1981 establishment of the AFP Bureau of Criminal Intelligence (ABCI), the charter of which required it to facilitate the exchange of intelligence between and among federal, state, and territory law enforcement organizations.

Many AFP operations conducted since the organization's founding have involved drug interdiction and immigration issues such as the falsification of passports. A 1995 investigation found that an Aum Shinrikyo compound in Western Australia had been used to develop the sarin nerve agent used by the criminal sect in its March attack on the Tokyo subway that year. The AFP also assisted Indonesian authorities with the forensic investigation conducted in the aftermath of the October 12, 2002, Bali discothèque bombing. The July 24, 2003, arrival of Ben McDevitt and fellow officers in Honiara marked further participation in regional law enforcement operations.[19] Those police personnel joined ten members of the New Zealand Police who had been on the islands since October 2002 as part of that nation's Solomon Islands Policing Project. Another 25 New Zealanders would

---

[19] AFP historical information in this and the previous paragraph drawn from Australian Federal Police (2004a).

Figure 4.1
Structure of the Australian Federal Police

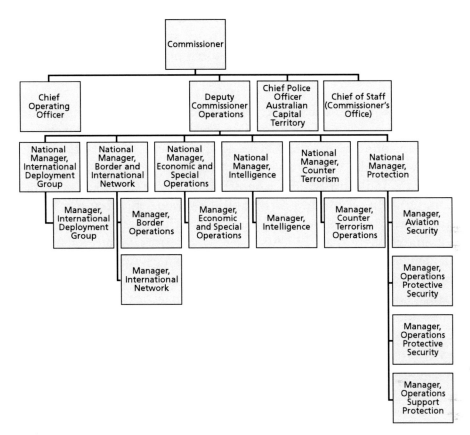

SOURCE: Adapted from Australian Federal Police (2004b, pp. 18–19). Greater detail
shown for Operations than for other areas.
RAND *MG551-4.1*

---

[20] New Zealand Police (2006).

[21] Australian Federal Police (2004b, p. 15).

addition to patrolling and assisting in the development of Royal Solomon Islands Police personnel, these officers ensured the safety of the prime minister and other public officials, conducted corruption and other criminal investigations, and (as noted with respect to the arrest of Harold Keke and other militia members) played a fundamental role in ending the reign of terror perpetrated by various gang and militia elements.

Provision of these services has not been without challenges. The aforementioned loss of an Australian policeman was but the worst of them. The number of personnel needed to support RAMSI meant that officers from the various states and territories were needed to assist their AFP and other nations' counterparts during the ongoing operation. Other missions drew further on the various organizations' infrastructures. A December 2003 agreement with Papua New Guinea committed more than 230 AFP, state, and territory police officers to an "enhanced cooperation program under which Australian officials would work side by side with Papua New Guineans in policing, law and justice and economic and public-sector management."[22] These commitments joined with others for deployments to Timor Leste (formerly East Timor) and Cyprus, precipitating the February 2004 founding of an International Deployment Group to help manage the many ongoing missions undertaken by the country's police.[23]

The demands and risks for law enforcement officers have continued in the years following their colleagues' initial arrival. Continued responsibilities have not allowed the dramatic decreases in personnel similar to those achieved by RAMSI's military arms. Despite the considerable progress made toward greater stability, violent demonstrations in Honiara that accompanied the parliament's appointment of a new prime minister in April 2004 resulted in injuries to 12 RAMSI police personnel.[24] Their continued role in developing Royal Solomon Islands Police capabilities promises many more years of service.

---

[22] Australian Federal Police (2004b, p. 15).

[23] Australian Federal Police (2004b, p. 15).

[24] Zinn (2006).

Nga Hoe Tuputupu-mai-tawhiti (The Paddles That Bring Growth from Afar): Aid Organizations and RAMSI

> The overarching goal of Australia's aid program in Solomon Islands is "a peaceful, well-governed and prosperous Solomon Islands." This goal will be pursued over the longer term through a mutual commitment with the Solomon Islands Government.
> —*Australian Agency for International Development (2006a, p. v)*

Much of both the initial and later success of RAMSI rests on the foundation provided by AusAID, NZAID,[25] and those with which these organizations worked in sustaining the Solomon Islander population and supporting a government on the verge of collapse. It was in the realm of support that the continuity so essential to building rested. The representatives of these organizations and Solomon Islanders who had been trained by them were in many cases the bases on which struggling governmental agencies were reconstructed and to which investigators turned when RAMSI sought to excise the corruption that plagued the renewal process.

AusAID and NZAID are administratively autonomous agencies within their respective nations' Departments of Foreign Affairs and Trade. Their missions include partnering with regional governments, nongovernmental organizations, and private-sector donors to effectively provide aid and build governmental capabilities in response to emerging challenges and during humanitarian crises. While focused on the Southern Pacific region for many of their undertakings, their charter has in recent years also included provision of assistance in Indonesia, East Timor, Iraq, Sudan, and Iran, to provide but a sampling.[26] The organizations' objectives in the Solomon Islands encompass far more than aid provision alone, as is evident in the following statement from AusAID's 2003–2004 annual report:

---

[25] Nga Hoe Tuputupu-mai-tawhiti, in the title of this section, is the Maori name for NZAID (New Zealand Aid, 2006).

[26] Australian Agency for International Development (2006b).

The Machinery of Government program is an essential component of RAMSI. Recognising the centrality of state building in
fragile states, the program seeks to address serious ongoing deficiencies in government functions through assistance to improve
the functioning of the public service, cabinet processes, accountability institutions, Parliament and elections.

Australia has assisted the Solomon Islands Government target
corruption and deliver comprehensive strategies for public
administration reform and management. Australian assistance
has been important in improving recruitment policies and procedures, as well as promoting transparency and accountability
in government. Major audit reports, for example, were tabled
in Parliament in 2005 for the first time in almost two decades.
Recent Australian assistance for Parliamentary reform, electoral
reform and a nationwide civic education program serves as part
of a broader strategy to strengthen Parliament and democratic
accountability.[27]

Two complementary aspects of this support characterize its application in practice. Both are in keeping with the overarching intentions
of RAMSI leaders and that operation's participating governments.
First, just as RAMSI is present at the invitation of and as a partner
with the government of the Solomon Islands, so too is the assistance
provided by these aid agencies a constantly cooperative, as opposed
to a RAMSI-unilateral, venture. This is true both of the original
design of support mechanisms and procedures as well as the nature of
execution. Development of capabilities in the law and justice sector
demonstrates this approach. In the words of AusAID, "Australia's assistance to the law and justice sector is guided by a new framework developed in conjunction with the Solomon Islands Government. A law and
justice program unit in the Ministry of Police, National Security, Justice and Legal Affairs is assuming responsibility for the management
of Australia's assistance to the sector. Australian support is aimed at

---

[27] Australian Agency for International Development (2006b).

equitable access to justice through efficient, affordable and accountable institutions."[28]

Second, both the nature and extent of the aid and other assistance provided remain within the self-imposed constraints of the mandate, i.e., RAMSI seeks to build the Solomon Islands' capacity for continued success, providing sufficient sustainment to its people and government until the establishment of that capacity without overreaching those limits to thereby create dependency.

These self-imposed limits do not preclude participating aid agencies from assisting across a broad scope of sectors and functions. Enhancing the islands' transportation, health, and education infrastructures; agricultural processes; forestry management; and land management practices are all on the agenda.[29] Recognizing that rural areas have in many instances been denied the fiscal resources necessary, aid organizations have participated in the RAMSI Budget Stabilization Program, an initiative to ensure that funding reaches provincial officials and programs supporting outlying arenas.[30]

In keeping with the overall strategy of RAMSI, all development programs seek to employ a whole of government approach through the provision of advice and side-by-side working relationships, as best suits the extent and character of the challenges at hand:

> Australia's development program in Solomon Islands is characterised by strong and innovative whole of government engagement through a range of Australian agencies, including the Australian Federal Police, the Australian Defence Force, the departments of Treasury, Finance and Administration and Attorney-General, the Australian Office of Financial Management, and the Australian Customs Service. This will continue, both through inline assistance—where expatriate personnel occupy positions within the partner government—and advisory assistance while capacity needs are high. But it will also be ongoing through links between

---

[28] Australian Agency for International Development (2006b).

[29] Australian Agency for International Development (2006b).

[30] Cox and Morrison (2004, p. 6).

institutions, strategic oversight and lateral coordination on a range of crosscutting program issues such as capacity building.[31]

While emphasizing this method from the perspective of Australian capabilities, the AusAID *Solomon Islands Transitional Country Strategy, 2006 to mid-2007*, from which this description comes, goes on to identify other entities assisting in Solomon Islands development. A partial list includes the World Bank, Asian Development Bank, United Nations, European Union, and, of course, the several nations participating in RAMSI.[32] AusAID cites 12 "Draft Principles for Good International Engagement in Fragile States" that guide its actions in providing and coordinating aid in circumstances such as those confronting the leadership and people of the Solomon Islands. Unsurprisingly, many reflect or are reflected in the policies that guide RAMSI across all facets of its mission:

1. Take context as the starting point. All fragile states require sustained international engagement, but analysis and action must be calibrated to particular country circumstances.

2. Move from reaction to prevention.

3. Focus on state-building as the central objective.

4. Align with local priorities and/or systems.

5. Recognise the political-security-development nexus. The political, security, economic and social spheres are interdependent: failure in one risks failure in all others.

6. Promote coherence between donor government agencies.

7. Agree on practical coordination mechanisms between international actors.

---

[31] Australian Agency for International Development (2006a, p. 5).

[32] Australian Agency for International Development (2006a, p. 13).

8. Do no harm. International actors should especially seek to avoid activities which undermine national institution-building, such as bypassing national budget processes or setting high salaries for local staff which undermine recruitment and retention in national institutions. Donors should work out cost norms for local staff remuneration in consultation with government and other national stakeholders.

9. Mix and sequence aid instruments to fit the context.

10. Act fast. . . .

11. . . . but stay engaged long enough to give success a chance.

12. Avoid pockets of exclusion.[33]

As already noted, AusAID was among the aid providers that retained a presence in the Solomon Islands even during the difficult months preceding RAMSI. That sustained presence had a direct impact on RAMSI anticorruption convictions through the provision of financial records during preliminary investigations. It furthermore sustained a base of Solomon Islands officials and aid officials able and dedicated to working together in the interest of continuing and improving governmental capabilities. Later RAMSI rotations have seen a dramatic reduction in the extent and influence of military involvement. The improvement in the security situation reflected by such a reduction has in turn allowed for a dramatic increase in the proportion of resources dedicated to building the nation's capabilities and improving the lot of its citizens. Aid agencies' continuous commitment at first served to sustain minimal national government functions in a time of crisis, then assisted in purging that government of those who impeded rebuilding

---

[33] Australian Agency for International Development (2006a, pp. 24–26). A more complete description of each principle appears in the original. Expansions on individual principles are provided here only when it is thought that the principle is not self-explanatory.

while ensuring that such reconstruction efforts addressed appropriate sectors of national life within the confines of the RAMSI mandate.

Effective law enforcement, aid, and other interagency undertakings require all participating organizations to demonstrate a spirit of cooperation and willingness to "walk around the table," the better to view all issues from others' as well as their own perspectives. Three areas merit special note in this regard, given their dramatic input in the success of RAMSI in its first years. Those are intelligence, command-and-control (C2) relationships, and the coordination of aid efforts.

Intelligence in Support of COIN and Other Stability Operations

Counterinsurgencies—and stability operations in general—share a fundamental need with routine police work and virtually any military operation: a need for quality intelligence. The primary parties of RAMSI all deployed capabilities to support their own intelligence requirements, but found that sharing intelligence was complicated by differences in approach; types of information needed; and the ways intelligence was employed in creating, analyzing, and disseminating resultant products. There was also the real danger of poorly coordinated intelligence initiatives resulting in crucial intelligence never reaching those most in need of it. The lesson is one long ago learned but too often overlooked in subsequent undertakings:

> Counterguerrilla warfare depends on intelligence gathering. Selective force must be based on precise information. To gather this information the government has to create an effective apparatus for civil-military co-operation. The soldier must settle into the policeman's territory for a long period of time and the two must work together. [Commander in Malaya General Gerald] Templer's insistence that every member of the armed forces, civil service and police was engaged in counterinsurgency produced a unified effort that led to victory. The insistence of some authorities that the United States military should not be involved in the drug war, which is a form of counterinsurgency, reflects the compartmentalized thinking that produces defeat.[34]

---

[34] Beckett and Pimlott (1985, p. 193).

Fortunately the issue in the Solomon Islands was less one of such compartmentalizing (or "stovepiping" in U.S. colloquial terms) than a belief that other agencies' intelligence was simply of a different sort than the police, military, or DFAT might require. Admiral Bonser recognized that "the processes the police and military use are different. They use intelligence for different purposes, and that can cause friction unless it is managed closely."[35] The Australian Army's Major Simon Monterola realized that an initial military, police, and DFAT willingness to operate virtually separate intelligence operations was a matter of not understanding what counterparts had to offer rather than indicative of any antipathy. From his perspective as a military intelligence officer, he saw that the police were at first not impressed with the need to coordinate military intelligence operations with their own, believing that "we're talking to the people every day." As time went on, however, the broader perspective taken by the army with respect to HUMINT and field intelligence in general provided valuable augmentation to what law enforcement officers were obtaining through their own procedures. Police tended to focus their intelligence efforts on specific criminal activities or groups; they found the wider military focus helpful as nationwide activities became the daily routine.[36] In turn, police contacts with local citizens and DFAT's strategic intelligence complemented the ADF's material.

Command and Control During the Early Months of RAMSI
The intelligence situation represented in microcosm greater differences in the ways in which the principal agencies conducted C2 functions. One individual, drawing on experience that provided an overarching perspective on the earlier phases of RAMSI, concluded,

> The C2 piece is weak as well. . . . I think somewhere in the interagency continuum there is a mid-place between centralization and decentralization, and in the Solomon Islands it was too decentralized. [The speaker draws a picture of a tent with two tables down

---

[35] Bonser (2005).

[36] Monterola (2005).

the opposite sides.] That's the way it was for weeks. The AFP on this side, the ADF on the other side, and no one in between, and never the twain shall meet. [One of the intelligence personnel there at the time] said it was a basket case. And I think it was successful because of the lack of a threat. . . . But as time went on, the C2 part got better. . . . At the top level it went well, but at the O3 [captain] and O4 [major] level [there continued to be problems]. . . . A policeman goes out, but the military has no idea where he is, and they are responsible for security. . . . When it's more risky, it'll make your eyes fall out of your head, but within two months, three months, it's better.[37]

Centralization and decentralization were somewhat in tension, in part because of the day-to-day C2 approaches taken by respective leaders. The police approach tended to be very decentralized, not a surprise given the dispersion of their personnel and outposts throughout the area of operations and the disparate nature of law enforcement tasks. Military operations reflected a middle ground. Junior leaders operated within well-defined bounds established by orders and mission statements, but they were expected to exercise judgment in keeping with their commander's intentions when executing situations requiring initiative. DFAT operations were the most reliant on decisions made by single individuals. Often, this was the ambassador or other senior representative (Nick Warner, in the case of RAMSI), who by the nature of his or her considerable experience is expected to make an appropriate judgment after being provided with the information available pertaining to the problem at hand.

Here again, the differences in intelligence approaches are demonstrative. The difficulty during the opening weeks of RAMSI was that the various intelligence processes were providing separate inputs without an overarching context; the whole therefore lacked the synthesis that would give decisionmakers a common intelligence picture.[38] As noted in the prior quotation, the various participants soon recognized the

---

[37] Anonymous interview.

[38] Hutcheson (2005b; 2005a, p. 49).

value in each other's approaches and thereafter better melded the individual parts into a more effective whole. The DFAT—and RAMSI—senior personage was key to this cohesion and the resultant improvement in intelligence effectiveness. One observer concluded, "There's a real malaise in the intelligence thing, but [Nick Warner] was won over. . . . It's so dependent on getting the right guy . . . which they did, but the process is lunacy."[39]

Civil-Military Coordination of Aid Efforts

The third area worthy of special note is CIMIC, the coordination of military operations with other governmental and nongovernmental agencies. There were no separate Australian Army CIMIC organizations during actions in East Timor. Little had changed in this regard as units deployed to the Solomon Islands, though the earlier contingency had firmly demonstrated a need to better coordinate the disparate parts that comprised the whole of support being provided to the country. These duties fell primarily to artillery officers who had received training for the civil-military mission, many of whom had fortunately served in CIMIC roles in Timor.[40] Their task was considerably eased in comparison with that demanded in the earlier venue, however. RAMSI benefited from the already-established presence of federal aid agencies and their resultant preparation to immediately assume responsibility for overseeing and orchestrating many components of the mission's support requirements. That AusAID had already been in the Solomon Islands for some months prior to RAMSI's arrival meant that it was in an excellent position to capitalize on the enhanced stability and security situation brought about by the arrival of police and military personnel. Army leaders quickly realized that their efforts to redress the CIMIC preparedness that had hindered efforts in Timor were largely unnecessary due to the capabilities already in place. They responded by quickly scaling back the numbers of military personnel originally assigned these duties.

---

[39] Anonymous interview.

[40] Flowers (2005); Kilcullen (2006b).

Subsequent problems in this regard were fairly minor ones. The International Red Cross, for example, wanted to put their symbol on all signs related to the highly effective weapon turn-ins being run by police and military personnel. RAMSI authorities denied the advertising initiative.[41] A potentially more harmful and notably frustrating shortfall resulted from selected agencies desiring to address special niche areas of interest. One observer found the problems with nongovernmental organizations (NGOs) worse in the Solomon Islands than any in previous personal experience due to the infighting that characterized the NGOs' claims to particular "turf" over which each would be responsible:

> The difficulties were with the NGOs that we had there. I'd never experienced—in Bosnia and elsewhere—this squabbling . . . even supplying sheets to the local hospital. You had to put everything through this bloody slow process. . . . "That's project number 213 with this organization and those sheets will be delivered in 12 weeks."[42]

While there were NGOs that provided excellent support, there were others whose members were too interested in addressing organizational or personal agendas to provide effective assistance to Solomon Islanders in need. It is here that CIMIC can help by establishing procedures that bypass private interests while capitalizing on the value added by competent organizations. CIMIC serves best as a coordinator and facilitator rather than as a provider of aid in its own right. Considerable skill is needed to properly manage these assets, given the voluntary and sometimes fragile nature of NGO participation during many undertakings. It is an area as of yet too often as much a source of frustration as a benefit to the indigenous population.

---

[41] Anonymous interview.

[42] Anonymous interview.

Concluding Thoughts Regarding Interagency Challenges

> Another element fundamental to success was that the principles supported each other with each other, presenting a united front to Canberra and their subordinates. When they sent something back to Canberra with the message that the "RAMSI principals all agree," it inevitably was supported. When there was disagreement, it was pandemonium back in Australia. Every once in a while someone in Canberra would cause problems and one of the principals would have to whack Canberra. It is critical that those at higher echelons not in theater and therefore with a lesser understanding of the situation not try to remote-control.
>
> —*Ben McDevitt, senior Australian Federal Police*
> *representative to RAMSI (2005a)*

Perhaps no element lent more to the success of RAMSI than getting the right man or woman for the job. Australia's selection of the senior members of RAMSI —the Big Three—was precisely what was needed to achieve the sought-after objectives.[43] The same can be said for many of those representing their organizations at lower echelons and the individuals chosen to participate on behalf of other agencies and nations. The understanding fostered during previous training and deployment relationships was one critical factor in reducing friction and establishing an initial common ground when working out problems. Yet it was the dedication to a common cause and the subjugation of personal and organizational egos by the Big Three that foremost set the tone for RAMSI. John Frewen's chief of staff, Major Charles Weller, expressed a view repeatedly articulated during author interviews: that coopera-

---

[43] John Frewen (2005b) noted that there were four principals initially, the fourth being Margaret Thomas of AusAID. However, the rapid rotation of AusAID leadership (three individuals during the first six months of RAMSI) and the early focus on security and restoration of the rule of law shifted emphasis to DFAT, AFP, and ADF. Frewen further explained that "as soon as the bad guys were gone, the attention shifted to aid," a point emphasized in the previous discussion of federal and private aid agencies that were part of or otherwise supported RAMSI.

tion "flowed down" to the echelons below these top leaders.[44] John Hutcheson, the CTF 635 commander during RAMSI's third military rotation, went further in emphasizing the value of carefully selecting the right people for the job: "The key to success . . . is the relationships you build right from the start, and with the agencies. You can spend a lot of time butting chests and not getting anything done. You need to pick the right personalities. . . . The individuals and the skills and talents they possess, but also their personalities."[45]

The right personalities were critical; there were other additional influences that underlay the effectiveness of this triumvirate. One was the undisputed status of each Big Three member as senior representative of his organization, whether DFAT, police, or military. Peter Cosgrove, as Australia's Chief of Defence Force during the origination of RAMSI, directed that Lt Col John Frewen be the only lieutenant colonel in the force, all other officers being subordinate to him. Cosgrove wanted to ensure that there was no doubt about who was in charge. The only exceptions to the rank stipulation were Colonel Paul Symon, who served in his advisory and liaison capacity to Nick Warner and was therefore not in the RAMSI chain of command; the commander of the *Manoora*; and others representing coalition militaries (e.g., Shaun Clarke, New Zealand air force) or having uniquely specialized skills.[46] All such exceptions appreciated the need for unity of command and did not challenge the status of Frewen or his successors in this regard. The situation nevertheless led to some unusual circumstances, e.g., Frewen had 54 majors subordinate to him. In the end, however, Cosgrove's intention served RAMSI well.[47]

---

[44] Charles Weller (2005).

[45] Hutcheson (2005b).

[46] Frewen (2005b); Bill Thomson (2005).

[47] At least one of those interviewed believed that the Australian Navy's Mark Bonser, being Frewen's immediate superior in Australia and the man responsible for managing joint assets as they readied to report to Lt Col Frewen, was another crucial element. Bonser, as other than an army officer, might have felt less compulsion to directly influence Frewen. The military chain of command was simple and clear (anonymous interview). In Frewen's words: "Nobody could give anyone in the military an order but me. I reported to Mark Bonser who reported directly to General Cosgrove" (Frewen, 2005b).

Nick Warner was the senior RAMSI official. Ultimately, it was his responsibility to make crucial decisions in instances of disagreement and to set policy on the ground. Both Warner and those working with him described his role as senior DFAT representative as one of coordinator rather than leader in the context envisioned during a military operation. Bluntly asked who was ultimately in charge, Warner's response reflected cognizance that this was his responsibility while emphasizing the communal nature of the operation's management:

> I was the boss, but I was coordinating. . . . It's sort of a unique position. I wasn't telling J. J. [Frewen] directly what to do with his troops or Ben what to do with his police. . . . We were making collective decisions. I was making decisions to make sure we were working in the same direction and that no activities went off the rails to threaten the operation more broadly. . . . Ben was the perfect person for that position. He was very experienced, a very good strategic thinker . . . and J. J. [Frewen] was a half-colonel, running 1,600 troops from five countries, and it worked.[48]

Ben McDevitt's previous observation regarding the unified front established by the Big Three characterized the approach encouraged by Warner and supported by his military and police counterparts. Chosen for their skills, granted considerable freedom of action, and better aware of local needs than any in remote capitals, the trio

> met at least daily, twice daily in the first weeks, to discuss events, combine plans and coordinate actions. . . . This had the effect of setting RAMSI policy from the top and ensured that we were all singing from the same sheet of music. It also helped with the coordination between the agencies. This common approach was also apparent in the media conferences that were conducted, as all three would be present. The CTF staff referred to this system as

---

[48] Warner (2005). The actual number of military personnel in Frewen's command was 1,800 at its peak.

the "triumvirate," and it was widely understood that we operated as part of a whole-of-government approach as a result.[49]

The united front generally presented to Canberra and the media also applied to the Big Three's relations with subordinates in the Solomon Islands. There was a single policy, a single message, agreed upon and supported by Warner, McDevitt, and Frewen. This cooperation tended to smother all but mundane interagency squabbles. That is not to imply there were not disagreements, but the principals sought to ensure that any that arose were not allowed to threaten the success of RAMSI.

Such cooperation demanded considerable adaptation by leaders and subordinates cast into roles rarely confronted in training or previous operations. With numbers far fewer than those of the soldiers, sailors, and airmen ensuring a secure environment, ultimately it was the police who would most immediately influence the reestablishment of the legitimacy and rule of law that were their priority functions. That meant that, tactically, it was the fewer than 300 police rather than the 1,800 military personnel who were in charge in the field.[50] The military's was a supporting role, despite the fact that its numbers far exceeded those of any other deployed agency. Such subordination is

---

[49] Bennett (2005a). David Kilcullen provides an interesting discussion of the difference between the U.S. *interagency* and Australian *whole of government* concepts:

> The U.S. term "interagency coordination" is subtly but importantly different from the Australian concept of "whole-of-government approach." These equate to the equivalent military concepts of "inter-services liaison" versus "joint operations"—one emphasizes independent parties coordinating with each other, the other focuses on the delivery of a combined effect. Few people in Australia, except those who have served with the US, use the term "interagency" unless talking to Americans. Instead, "whole of government" language is widely used and embedded in all Australian government departments. This allows a very rapid generation of a "one team, one fight" ethos when working together. (Kilcullen, 2006b)

This distinction is an interesting—and important—one. It would appear that the many calls for greater interagency cooperation during U.S. operations seek what is encompassed in the "whole of government" conceptualization rather than coordination or cooperation alone. The distinction is worth noting explicitly when defining future requirements.

[50] The values are from Warner (2004a).

not commonplace for U.S. military men and women; failure to adapt in the exceptions has undermined or led to outright mission failure in some instances.[51] It was also a challenge for some of the soldiers participating in RAMSI, as related by John Hutcheson:

> A final lesson from the Solomon Islands mission was the constant need to reinforce to soldiers the the military was operating in support of the police. In the Solomon Islands this situation meant that the PPF [participating police forces] dictated that tempo and type of operations conducted—which for some soldiers was initially difficult to accept. For example, from the outset of RAMSI there was a clear need to develop an extensive military patrolling program in order to provide a secure environment. The adoption of an immediate patrolling regime was the initial advice given by senior military officers to their PPF counterparts. However, a patrol system is not how the PPF wished to conduct initial operations. In such a situation the best that a military commander can do is to advise, perhaps remonstrate, and then try to influence decisions that have an impact on the welfare and safety of his deployed troops. In future RAMSI-style missions, it will be important in force preparation courses and in-theatre reception packages to ensure that the conditions military personnel are likely to meet in an inter-agency operation are clearly outlined from the outset. This is vital in order to pre-empt any surprise, disappointment or frustration that might develop concerning each agency's different techniques. There remains, as always, a need for soldiers to be constantly aware of the character of any mission involving civilian agencies.[52]

---

[51] There are notable exceptions, e.g., British Army patrols are subordinate to police during operations in Northern Ireland. David Kilcullen expands on this, noting that

> this directly reflects British Commonwealth—including Australian and NZ—doctrine for counterinsurgency, which emphasizes police primacy as practiced in Malaya, Northern Ireland and other operations. This is a key fundamental in Australian doctrine and military members would have been familiar with it from training. (Kilcullen, 2006b)

[52] Hutcheson (2005a, pp. 53–54).

That the Australian military did adapt, and that the AFP, DFAT, and other agencies did not abuse their status of supported role was fundamental to mission accomplishment. RAMSI leaders actively promoted this cooperation, and helped to overcome some initial friction between various agency representatives, through interagency sporting and social events.[53]

At times, evidence of which was the supporting or supported agency was a matter of nuance; military staff personnel would sit in the AFP area of the operations center rather than vice versa, for example.[54] Cooperation was enhanced by physically collocating headquarters functions. Mark Bonser felt that "the fact that they were forced to work together physically . . . meant that they had to come together. . . . I think that helps you to overcome the process problems . . . the fact that you've not been able to set up your own bits of turf and empires."[55] In other instances, it was a matter of employing a diplomatic approach rather than an overbearing one. Army planning was a strong point, not a surprise given the extent to which it is a centerpiece of military training. Charles Weller recalled his commander's approach in offering plans to other RAMSI participants, one that provided input without unnecessary assertiveness or pride in authorship. Asked what he believed were the keys to the operation's success, he responded,

> The army was willing to take a supporting role. They would develop plans and forward them to J. J. Frewen, the military commander, who would take them to the police and other agencies. He presented the plans to the other agency representatives with a soft touch, e.g., "Hey, we're thinking of this." The representatives would take them and come back a few weeks later, often with approaches very similar to what the army proposed initially.[56]

---

[53] Hutcheson (2005a, p. 52).

[54] Hutcheson (2005b).

[55] Bonser (2005).

[56] Weller (2005).

In the end, the common dedication to a single cause served as a foundation that guided individuals and organizations and promoted cooperation. Military and police alike understood that it would ultimately have to be the Solomon Islands police who guaranteed the population's freedom from intimidation and harm. Thus, although RAMSI's army forces had law enforcement authority equal to that of participating police representatives, the soldiers never exercised that authority. They served in a backup role to their law enforcement colleagues, supporting the development of RSIP legitimacy by avoiding direct involvement in arrests. New Zealand Army Major Vern Bennett explained:

> A key consideration for the CTF was that the military was not in charge but we were very much working towards the aims and plans of the PPF. In that regard, we conformed to their tactical deployment patterns and went on patrol when they did—we did not conduct independent patrols or activities. This was a major change from East Timor, for example, which was more of a "classic" military security mission where we as military forces established our patrol routines, objectives, etc. In the Solomon Islands, the military did not conduct any activity outside of PPF requests for assistance or as part of combined activities with the PPF.

> The issue of AOs [areas of operations] was based on the requirement to support the PPF and therefore work with them. In this regard, it was imperative that PPF and CTF worked in combined areas and did not have separate systems of AOs, as this would have negated the effect that we were trying to achieve. With regard to the issue of national AOs, it should be remembered that the CTF was a small force and that tying areas to nations would have quickly dissipated our strength. Furthermore, the CTF had a rotation plan established in order to keep the troops fresh, maintain forces for contingencies and to avoid the overreliance of a local population on the CTF instead of the PPF. This was another means of establishing and maintaining the primacy of

the PPF, as they would establish the longer-term relations in an area while the CTF forces that rotated through would provide the necessary support and security.[57]

The aforementioned differences in language (police-speak versus military-speak) and procedures, combined with the excessively short mission preparation time, meant that a seamless integration of operations was impossible. The issue of what conditions would alter the command relationship (i.e., when the military would take charge should the tactical situation demand it) was never fully resolved. This did not pose a significant threat given the ultimate lack of resistance to RAMSI's authority. In a less permissive environment, however, not knowing when the responsibility for command shifted could have been a costly shortfall. Such a transfer, often necessary suddenly due to an ambush or similar unexpected appearance of a threat, can be difficult. It should therefore be clearly understood by all involved and rehearsed prior to mission initiation. That these questions extended into the army's second RAMSI rotation is a notable shortcoming, albeit one that by necessity would have been addressed had conditions so demanded.[58] Threat concerns aside, the extent of interagency cooperation and willingness to build understanding continually through on-the-job training after deployment to theater offers lessons for any agency undertaking COIN operations in the future.

RAMSI's success was in considerable part also attributable to an exchange of effective liaison officers between the agencies. This started at the most senior level, with Colonel Paul Symon providing Nick Warner with an accurate understanding of armed forces perspectives and motivations. Liaison between the many agencies at lower echelons was no less important. Here, again, the power of personality was recognized and the right person was often found for the job. Symon brought

---

[57] Bennett (2005a). The reason for East Timor being of a more classic military nature is at least in part explained by the police component assigned to that mission as affiliates of UNAMET rather than INTERFET. The police component departed in August 1999 and was not replaced until late December of that year, leaving the military with the responsibility of assuming its duties (Kilcullen, 2006b).

[58] Anonymous interview.

considerable skills to his position, having formerly served as Australia's senior military observer in the Middle East and later as a liaison officer in East Timor.[59] Lieutenant Colonel Luke Foster's valuable service as Australia's military representative to the Solomon Islands government from January 2002 to January 2005 has been noted. He used his considerable knowledge of the local situation to act as an intermediary between the RSIP and ADF.[60] Though the initial Australian Army liaison to the AFP was dedicated and hardworking, interagency relations were further improved when a major who had once been a police officer assumed the coordination task. Charles Weller described the importance of finding the right man for the job in this specific instance:

> A very positive step forward took place in week four. Major Rowan Jayawardene joined CJTF 635. J. J. [Frewen] and I immediately recognized that he was the right man to act as the liaison officer between the army and the AFP. Rowan had been in the infantry, left the army to serve seven years with the Queensland Police Force, then returned to army active duty. He therefore provided a "translation service. He spoke 'copper.'" The captain in the job at the time of Rowan's arrival had been doing an acceptable job, but he was still learning both how to be a liaison officer and "the language" at the same time. "It's all about liaison officers."[61]

Similarly, the AFP's choice as their representative to the army had once been an Australian Army warrant officer.[62]

Some of these assignments may have been serendipitous, hardly the manner in which such choices should be made. Most, however, were deliberate, reflecting keen insight on the part of those determining the assignments. Critical under any circumstances, these choices were immensely valuable given the brief time the various agencies had

---

[59] Londey (2004, pp. 237–238).

[60] Foster (2005).

[61] Weller (2005). Portions not in quotation marks are paraphrased.

[62] Bennett (2005a).

to work together between notification and actual deployment to the islands.[63]

There was room for future improvement despite the considerable successes with respect to liaison between various agencies. Major Vern Bennett found the previously highlighted military relationship with civilian aid organizations one potential area meriting improvement. CIMIC staff (which consisted of military personnel) coordinated relations between the military and development-assistance agencies, but that coordination did not reach the same level of effectiveness as that between the military and police.[64] The vital role of these organizations and the need to incorporate them into a broader vision of interagency cooperation is evident in a decision to assume the calculated risk of allowing International Committee of the Red Cross (ICRC) representatives to see RAMSI's rules of engagement (ROE). James Watson, an Australian Army lawyer who would join the AFP after his tour with RAMSI, recommended to John Frewen that the military establish an environment of open exchange with those nongovernmental agencies sharing the burden of rebuilding the Solomon Islands' shaken society. Watson reasoned that the ROE release would not reveal anything not already known by members of threat organizations, e.g., that RAMSI personnel had the right to defend themselves with lethal force.[65] Frewen agreed despite some pressures to do otherwise, believing that "it would reinforce that we were there to do business, but it would also reinforce our openness with the ICRC."[66]

While it is hard to overstate the value of effective liaison officers, these individuals cannot replace predeployment interagency training and coordination. James Watson recalled providing classes to a group of police officers before the operation's initiation. Watson ventured beyond his assigned topic of ROE when he realized that the law enforcement personnel were unfamiliar with many aspects of military

---

[63] Bennett (2005a).

[64] Bennett (2005a).

[65] Watson (2005b).

[66] Frewen (2005b).

activities, including the weapons the police might have to employ if their own malfunctioned in a combat situation. Most of his students "had never used a Glock before [the 9mm Glock 19 service pistol used in the army]. They didn't realize that when it's loaded there's one up the spout. You pull the trigger and it [fires]."[67]

The trust built between the various RAMSI organizations infiltrated daily operations and influenced decisions later found to have vital impact on the ultimate success of early security efforts. James Watson's position as an army lawyer allowed him to straddle the police and military communities. He thought that the restraint exercised by law enforcement officers had lessons for the soldier. Watson found police personnel better "able to move around the continuum of force. Soldiers saw only one direction to go: up. . . . There were times when the police would just stand back during an incident. They had been trained in that regard."[68] The military's bias for action proved to be less necessary in defeating the Solomon Islands' counterinsurgency than did police patience and less aggressive approaches. Ben McDevitt's letters to Harold KeKe and the subsequent patience demonstrated by the Big Three during continued written and face-to-face negotiations are prime examples. Both Nick Warner and John Frewen thought their police counterpart's negotiation skills vital to the early successes of RAMSI. Frewen was at first not convinced of the value of the more patient approach, but he soon became a believer, finding that "people trusted us. The bad guys trusted us. We [the army] wanted to grab Harold and trust be damned. But Ben said no. Ben was an experienced police negotiator" and it was his more restrained methods that both Frewen and Warner credit with bringing KeKe into RAMSI custody on August 13, 2003, day 21 of the coalition's deployment, following several face-to-face meetings with the Big Three in a small church in the Weathercoast area.[69] Many consider the faction leader's

---

[67] Watson (2005b).

[68] Watson (2005b).

[69] Frewen (2005b); McDevitt (2005b).

bloodless surrender the most important event of the first 12 months of deployment.[70]

The considerable number of nations, other governmental, and nongovernmental agencies involved helps to explain the rather extraordinary number of military officers subordinate to Lt Col Frewen during the initial RAMSI deployment. That he had 54 subordinates of major rank means that there was a major for approximately every 32 soldiers. A number of these soldiers were also captains or lieutenants, meaning that the ratio of officers to enlisted personnel in the force was far higher than would generally be the case. The reasons are not difficult to ascertain. The need for able liaison personnel is one. The presence of aviation units (with officer pilots); the requirement to coordinate logistical support to the many organizations supporting RAMSI operations and indigenous personnel; and the staff capabilities essential to orchestrate ongoing military security, law enforcement, civil support, and multinational and interagency activities all required officer involvement in considerable numbers. This officer-heavy force structure has several implications for other stability or COIN undertakings. Demands for near-instantaneous orchestration of assets on arrival in an area of operations and for the expertise essential in determining the types, quantities, and prioritization of resources crucial to mission success will favor

---

[70] McDevitt's qualifications and background certainly helped to identify him as a wise choice for the AFP lead during the initial RAMSI deployment: "Ben McDevitt, a former paratrooper, is now one of the Assistant Commissioners of the Australian Federal Police. Identified as a leader at a young age, Ben rose through the ranks to serve as the youngest commander of crime operations. Ben's family has a history of service and is the longest servicing family in the [Australian Capital Territory]" (National Australia Day Council, 2005). (The same site also notes that McDevitt "was awarded the Cross of the Solomon Islands which is the second highest award in the country" for his services with RAMSI and as a deputy commissioner in the RSIP.) McDevitt himself remarks that he

> spent many years as a senior investigator, particularly around major crimes, and as such I think developed considerable talent at negotiation. In addition, I also was a member of the Federal Police special operations team for a number of years and was a trained hostage negotiator. The third contributing aspect was that for two years (1994–96) I was the chief defensive skills instructor for the Australian Federal Police. In this role I developed and delivered instructional packages on subjects including "dealing with difficult people," "dealing with persons suffering mental illnesses," and "basic negotiation." (McDevitt, 2006)

an officer-heavy initial deployment. General Cosgrove's recognition that unity of command would facilitate that success was a significant insight that likely was fundamental to the operation's early accomplishments. The rapidity with which stability was restored allowed redeployment of the bulk of the military force—officers included—within the first year, thereby minimizing what could have been a severe strain on armed forces with limited manpower assets and several other ongoing regional and worldwide commitments at the time of RAMSI's initiation. The pre-RAMSI presence of AusAID in the country and the related ability of its personnel to fairly easily assume responsibility for building local capabilities was an advantage. Such a smooth realignment during the transition from early stability restoration to nation-building and sustainment demonstrates the effective interagency cooperation that underlay both RAMSI's continued advance toward its objectives and the ability of participating organizations to meet other strategic objectives beyond those in the Solomon Islands. This realignment was unquestionably abetted by the number of officers available to rapidly and effectively transfer their responsibilities to other agency representatives pending the military downsizing.

An additional key to RAMSI's interagency success is the Australian and New Zealand use of the interdepartmental committee (IDC) system to bring representatives of participating organizations together in the Australian capital. DFAT's First Assistant Secretary of the Pacific and Middle East Branch, Ric Wells, oversaw the IDC operation in Canberra.[71] He gave lead-nation Australia a single point for coordinating interagency issues, thereby dramatically reducing the likelihood that critical questions forwarded from the Solomon Islands would be lost in the bureaucracy or mishandled by agency representatives not as familiar with local concerns as those working directly with RAMSI. The importance of this link between those deployed and the capital is clear in the comments of an individual long familiar with the Solomon Islands and RAMSI:

---

[71] Anonymous interview.

I continue to believe that a fundamental reason the operation worked so well in the first year, and continues to function well, is the tight links that exist between Canberra and Honiara, to which Wellington now feeds into; and in the first year in particular, the relationship of trust between Nick Warner and Ric Wells was as important as similar relationships on the ground in Honiara.[72]

Avoiding Future Interagency Shortfalls

Despite the success of RAMSI and the interagency operations supporting it, there is recognition that resting on past accomplishments will leave problems unaddressed. New Zealander Vern Bennett and Australian Mark Bonser agree that "if the agencies had spent more time working together before they deployed, it would have been good" in terms of redefining the nature of relationships before exercising them in an active theater.[73] They are certainly not alone. Such preliminary preparation should include school and operational exchange programs between organizations likely to find themselves side-by-side during future ventures (assignments similar to those that resulted in many military personnel from participating nations having worked together previously). The exchanges would ideally incorporate formal training, plans development, and other functions effective in familiarizing various organizations' representatives with the workings of the host organization and preparing on-the-shelf plans in readiness for potential contingencies. John Hutcheson is another who approves of initiatives such as these, recommending that common planning procedures be developed and shared to facilitate greater operational effectiveness.[74] These are all valuable and viable recommendations, made the more so if the respective organizations track participants and later select them when deployments occur.

---

[72] Anonymous interview.

[73] Bennett (2005a).

[74] Hutcheson (2005b).

Building and Maintaining the Multinational Team

> Although many professional soldiers resist what they see as the constabulary function inherent in peace operations, it is a job that realistically only soldiers can do—as only they can bring, or threaten to bring, sufficient force to bear to enforce security.
>
> —*Alan Ryan (2000)*

> The multinational flavor to the RAMSI mission, . . . I think it was a single component of the success of the mission. . . . If we had just gone in there without them, I don't think it would have been a success. . . . The success is more about the moral success.
>
> —*Lieutenant Colonel John J. Frewen,*
> *Commander, CTF 635 (2005b)*

In its role as lead nation, Australia immediately recognized that its neighbors in the South Pacific had many capabilities that would strengthen RAMSI. Some of those capabilities related to language: other regional island nations shared indigenous languages or dialects with those in the Solomon Island communities. Some capabilities were cultural in another sense: customs and Melanesian social mores, largely unfamiliar to Australia's soldiers (other than those of Aboriginal background), were first nature to those with cultures similar to the Solomon Islanders'. Still others were political; the wide participation demonstrated regional unity in supporting the effort to address the nation's challenges. It was important that the force came at the invitation of the Solomon Islands leadership, but a more demographically representative soldiery assisted in neutralizing propaganda efforts attempting to capitalize on the makeup of RAMSI forces. Recall that military representation included men and women from Australia, New Zealand, Papua New Guinea, Fiji, and Tonga, and that the police force had law enforcement officers from those and another five nations in addition: Samoa, Fiji, Kiribati, Cook Islands, and Nauru.[75] Australians had

---

[75] "RAMSI Leaders Brief Pacific Neighbors" (2004).

assisted in training the militaries and police of many of these nations. The resultant relationships served to enhance cooperation and understanding, promote the use of common operating procedures, and provide the opportunity for future coalitions to more effectively interact with virtually any population found in the region. Participation by the many regional nations was critical to capitalizing on this potential; it also resulted in a redefinition of what the minimum size of a nation's effective representation could be. Lieutenant Colonel Quentin Flowers, second commander of CTF 635, initially believed that dealing with units of less-than-company strength would present significant logistical and control issues. He was pleasantly surprised to find himself wrong, discovering that leaders could integrate a platoon into RAMSI operations to positive effect.[76]

Figure 4.2
Papua New Guinea Soldiers Prepare to Deploy to the Solomon Islands

SOURCE: Photo courtesy of the Government of Australia, Department of Defence, Operation Anode photo gallery. Used with permission.
RAND MG551-4.2

---

[76] Flowers (2005).

The Australians drew on their considerable previous experience in Papua New Guinea, East Timor, and elsewhere as they attempted to mold an effective multinational team. East Timor was a particularly rich source of lessons in studying the challenges of heading a coalition. A passage that once again brings the challenge of effective communications to the fore demonstrates that interagency relations are not alone in presenting challenges in this regard:

> The problem of language was probably the greatest challenge to the cohesion of the force. . . . Even the Irish contingent commander pointed out that he had struggled to understand the briefings at the start. He noted that:

> "It is a terrible thing to struggle at a brief, especially when you are new and you are learning the procedures and you are just not quite sure what was actually said. I would wonder how the other Asian countries were feeling. . . . The Australians certainly speak much faster than we would speak ourselves and there certainly is a process of addressing their own in a brief and it is got by the participants in the brief [making] eye contact, nodding their heads—I understand, I understand. I would think that the briefer maybe should look away from those people and look to the blank faces that may be there."

> Three Thai colonels interviewed in Dili supported this perception, arguing that "the basic problem is language—we don't always understand what you are saying in English." They estimated that the Asian officers, in particular, understood only half of what was said at briefings and conferences, and they believed that Australian officers giving briefings appeared unaware of the issue. The colonels pointed out that the method of briefing needed to be adjusted to the audience, and that Australian officers tended to focus on the message and not on "reading" their audience. Their suggestions included reducing jargon, paying more attention to the level of comprehension exhibited by non–English speakers, and slowing down the presentations. This last point was of particular importance at the end of the briefings when questions were solicited. The rapid pace at which Australian briefings were

"wrapped up" posed major problems for the Asian officers. They were still formulating questions, and when asked for questions, tended to remain silent out of politeness rather than slow down the process.[77]

James Watson found that the "lesson of language" was one that needed to be relearned, at least by some. His was the responsibility to instruct multinational representatives regarding ROE much as he had the AFP, as described earlier. Watson became concerned when he distributed the OfOf (orders for opening fire) cards on which the lethal force provisions of the ROE appeared. The lack of comprehension on the part of his Papua New Guinea students (soldiers who would later prove notably effective in the Solomon Islands) was obvious. He quickly realized that language was the issue and arranged to have the OfOf cards translated from English. Watson recognized, as have so many working in a multinational environment, "It's all about language, language, language."[78]

There were other challenges in the multinational realm, designation of responsibilities among them. RAMSI leaders broke with accepted procedures on what proved to be an insightful means of resolving the problem. Differences in doctrine, equipment, ROE, and other operational variables suggest that assigning participating nations their own areas of operation was a wise way to minimize the frictions that can arise when integrating units from different nations. That was the procedure employed in East Timor; it is also the one currently used in Iraq. Those leading RAMSI instead adapted the integrated approach employed previously during TMG and PMG operations in Bougainville.[79] The approach involves disadvantages as well as benefits, however. Several participating nations' police and military contingents were of insufficient size to staff and support separate areas of responsibility unilaterally. RAMSI leaders further realized that assigning discrete segments of territory can result in the development of

---

[77] Ryan (2000, pp. 91–93).

[78] Watson (2005b).

[79] Kilcullen (2006b).

virtual fiefdoms, areas in which standards, messages, and means of interfacing with the public and local authorities take on a character influenced more by the responsible nation than by coalition objectives. Unity of message and dedication to common goals were key underpinnings of RAMSI; consistent police training procedures, legitimacy messages, and uniformly professional standards were carefully cultivated as part of the operation's larger intention to rebuild a viable governing capability. General Cosgrove made it clear that agency and multinational operations were to be fully integrated.[80] This required the considerable skill of leaders at the lowest tactical echelons; it was these men and women who had to lubricate the inevitable frictions by encouraging cooperation and compromise. It was also these individuals who ultimately combined the best capabilities of each organization to give RAMSI a highly flexible structure, one that nearly always resulted in at least one member of a patrol being able to communicate effectively with members of the population. The results were fundamental to coalition success as perceived by Solomon Islanders and the international community. Little wonder that Cosgrove believed that "the decisions of junior leaders and the actions of their small teams can influence the course of international affairs" as never before.[81]

Multinational command relationships at times presented unusual twists. Cooperation among the various countries was by and large exceptionally good, in part due to the previously mentioned familiarity the various contingent leaders had with one another. Though never to the extent that they seriously interfered with the counterinsurgency effort, there were still occasional anomalies that caused frustration. New Zealand's Group Captain Shaun Clarke initially offered his country's helicopters to the CTF 635 commander in an operational control (OPCON) relationship. This was considered appropriate given New Zealand's commitment to the mission, but it became apparent that unqualified adherence to an OPCON association meant that New Zealand national taskings (such as aviation support for the nation's visiting Minister of Defence and journalists) were subject to Australian-

---

[80] Frewen (2005b).

[81] Ryan (2000, p. 72).

led CTF approval. While the issue led to no significant operational problems, the potential for conflicts of interest were acknowledged. Certain caveats to the CTF's control authority were subsequently agreed to, ensuring that the overall mission always had primacy but that approval of selected New Zealand national taskings was not solely a matter of CTF discretion. A similar situation arose with New Zealand's army units, which were also in an OPCON status to the CTF 635 commander. A strict interpretation of OPCON meant that regaining control of soldiers for support of the occasional national humanitarian assistance mission could require more extensive coordination than should have been necessary. The issue was resolved via CIMIC coordination.[82]

Clarke discovered that while New Zealand had offered its forces to the commander of CTF 635 in an OPCON status, Royal Australian Navy (RAN) and Royal Australian Air Force (RAAF) assets were provided in "direct support." This meant that the RAN and RAAF had a greater degree of control over their forces than OPCON would have provided. In short, New Zealand had provided the CTF commander greater control than he had been given by his own air and naval services. The matter was resolved in Australia, but once again the short preparation time had resulted in less-than-desirable initial coordination and in frictions that could have had more severe consequences in a less benign environment or had patience been less forthcoming.[83]

Such misunderstandings require tolerance on the part of all parties involved. There is, on the one hand, the need for unity of effort and unity of message; the greater the discrepancy between the two, the greater the chances of alienating the local population and undermining the counterinsurgency effort as a whole. There is, however, also the need to recognize that different nations and agencies will wish to emphasize their own priorities when executing humanitarian missions or communicating with citizens back home. It is therefore necessary to structure command relationships and design guidance in such a way as to stay the desired course while providing leeway for individual nations

---

[82] Clarke (2005).

[83] Clarke (2005).

or organizations to adapt to the direction provided. Relations with the media provide a case in point. New Zealand's information-access policy was more open than that established by Australia. Reporters from Auckland, Wellington, and elsewhere in the home islands were regularly flown into the Solomon Islands on C-130 Hercules aircraft, a sore point with Australian members of CTF 635 who suffered complaints from their own media, which was refused such consideration.[84]

All participants suffered inconveniences and frustrations on occasion. Lieutenant Colonel Frewen's concern that an influx of relatively well-paid soldiers could a have dramatic and negative impact on the local economy was mentioned in Chapter One. He directed that no soldiers shop in Solomon Island stores or buy anything from the local population until the economy showed signs of being able to bear the influx of cash that liberalizing such policies would have. The policy, thought well advised by most of Frewen's Australian officers, was less popular with those from other countries due to the "no exceptions" manner in which it was enforced and the fact that it did not apply to police personnel (who did not fall under Frewen's command, worked at remote outposts at the end of sometimes very long supply lines, and whose numbers were far fewer than the military's). As one member of another nation's military contingent noted, they supported the policy, "but buying a fruit from across the fence from a snotty-nosed 10-year-old is hardly going to disrupt the economy."[85] There were similar issues regarding CTF 635 uniform policies. Participants interviewed admitted that these and similar disagreements amounted to little more than annoyances, disagreements that would have been overlooked entirely had the operation confronted a more active threat. Yet, many also pointed out that deployments are difficult enough without the introduction of avoidable problems. The need to develop memorandums of understanding before arrival in theater was a requirement often cited by many of those interviewed. While these can be helpful and are desirable, time constraints may preclude completing such arrangements before deployment. Further, it is important to note that no writ-

---

[84] Clarke (2005).

[85] Anonymous interview.

ten agreement should replace the reasoned judgment of good leaders on the ground.

As in the case of interagency operations, the multinational intelligence arena was a source of controversy. The problem interestingly seems to have been one spawned by Australian concerns about maintaining intelligence-exchange relationships with the United States. As a New Zealand officer serving with RAMSI explained in addressing access issues applicable to operations in Iraq, Afghanistan, and elsewhere,

> Intelligence was a real problem. . . . [Interview question: Were other nations upset because they were not allowed into the headquarters due to intelligence concerns?] Yeah, that definitely would have been the case. . . . The Americans will sit down with you at the SIPRNET [Secret Internet Protocol Router Network] and give you the information you need, but there's this whole thing with the Australians to preserve this relationship with the Americans, which is very important. . . . They [the Australians] give it this 10 percent extra to make sure they don't f— it up. . . . So, our closer friend [Australia] is more exclusive. . . . Politically, that lies at [the base of] most of the problems we have between the two of us. . . . The consequence of mucking up the intelligence relationship with the Americans is more important than the relationship between us. . . . It's got to be fixed. We're too close.[86]

It should be noted that these problems were not restricted to issues relating to U.S.-source intelligence materials alone. Demonstrating that other nations also need to reconsider their intelligence procedures, it was the denial of access by other RAMSI military representatives to the Australian Defence Restricted Network (DRN) and Defence Secret Network (DSN) that caused much in the way of frustration. The aggravation was very similar in character to that experienced by those working with the United States in Iraq. Imagery of Solomon Islands landing zones was not releasable to New Zealand personnel because it was posted on the DSN, despite being unclassified. A lim-

---

[86] Anonymous interview.

ited number of New Zealanders were provided access to the DSN after high-level negotiations between the two countries, but that access was not granted until close to the end of the first RAMSI military rotation.[87] The consequences of this denial could have been severe given a more robust threat. Regardless of the countries involved, such issues require resolution well before deployment, as access, or lack thereof, significantly affects planning as well as execution in the field.

Ultimately, the multinational challenges confronting RAMSI leaders were overcome. An observation made by a historian describing operations in East Timor still held valid for the Solomon Islands, however, and it reflects that there is need for further improvement during future missions:

> One factor that did shape the operational culture of the force was a degree of self-consciousness by HQINTERFET that this was an Australian-dominated mission. As Lieutenant Colonel Mark Wheeler, a New Zealander, put it:

> Ninety per cent of the time I think that you've done marvelously well and then ten per cent of the time I've got really frustrated when the Australian-centric view . . . or the Australian flavour overrides anything else where it needn't have. You are such a dominating force here that everyone knows that this is Australian-led and you don't need to reinforce that.

> This observation was repeated by a number of officers who otherwise had nothing but praise for the professionalism of Australian staff work and the support that was provided. It does appear that the DJFHQ [Deployable Joint Force Headquarters] has some way to go before it can really claim to "think combined."[88]

Wheeler's observations hold lessons for the United States. Rarely evident from a hemisphere's distance, Australia's role in the South Pacific is surprisingly like that of America's in the world: Australia is

---

[87] Anonymous interview.

[88] Ryan (2000, pp. 101–102).

the biggest player in the neighborhood and acts the part. Size has its advantages. There is also the danger of being perceived as unnecessarily domineering. That the Australian Army publishes historian Alan Ryan's frank observations and otherwise seeks to learn from past contingencies is commendable and reflective of an organization willing to learn and adapt. The U.S. military does likewise. The real value is in applying the lessons effectively.

Forming and Seizing the Moral High Ground: Shaping Indigenous Perspectives

> The communists are not slow to make propaganda capital out of all excesses committed by the government, with the result that most search-and-clear operations, by creating more communists than they kill, become in effect communist recruiting drives.
> —*Robert Thompson (1970)*

> The requirement for everyone from the most junior soldier to Warner to be on message was emphasized. It was a real success.
> —*Lieutenant Colonel James Bryant, Australian Army (2005b)*

RAMSI participants benefited tremendously from their familiarity with the Solomon Islands. The experiences gained by military, police, diplomatic representatives, and others while serving on the IPMT; insightful analyses by military attaches; and other government, aid, or commercial undertakings of greater or lesser duration present many opportunities to learn about the Solomon Islands population's needs, the problems underlying those requirements, and the character of potential threats.

Equally important: The leaders and those working in the field took advantage of these resources. Nick Warner and others in leadership roles knew what challenges confronted them and the social interrelationships that underpinned the corruption in the Solomon Islands government. This understanding allowed RAMSI to analyze the tangled webs of vice, determine their critical nodes and vulnerabilities, and thus strike with an effectiveness that kept the coalition in control of events, all while building and maintaining the desired relationships with members of the Solomon Islands government and population. Such knowledge also provided the means to properly design and tailor communications released by the coalition. The excellent intelligence set the preconditions for maintaining unity of message. All parties— internal and external to the Solomon Islands—could refer to speeches presented by the Big Three, view public affairs announcements by the many participating agencies and nations, or talk to the police officer or soldier on the street and receive consistent reinforcement of RAMSI themes:[89]

- RAMSI is committed to long-term rebuilding and maintenance of security.
- It is police in the RSIP on whom the population should rely for protection.
- Weapons are illegal and any Solomon Islander with a firearm is a criminal and foe of the people.
- Corruption at any level will no longer be tolerated.

The new standards applied to everyone, Solomon Islander and RAMSI participant alike. Those supporting the rejuvenation of the nation were rewarded. Barring previous participation in criminal activities, theirs was a more secure daily environment. They were permitted to keep their jobs. Their children could go to school. There would be no tolerance for those refusing to recognize the changed state of affairs or for those who had previously victimized the citizenry. Their future was one of trial with subsequent dismissal and imprisonment if convicted. Ben McDevitt's rapid action to remove those abusing their privileges as

---

[89] The idea of developing and conducting an "education campaign," "information operations," or "psychological operations" elicited resistance from a few RAMSI participants on occasion. Lt Col John Hutcheson, the commander of CTF 635 during its third rotation, explained, "Some other agencies thought this was unsavory, so I said we need to come up with a 'communications strategy.' And they said, 'Oh, a communications strategy. We need that'" (Hutcheson, 2005b).

police officers signaled instant change; a willingness to hear complaints regarding members of RAMSI itself reinforced that justice applied to all. (Fortunately, the latter were little more than irritant in character, e.g., a resident of the town of Gizo complaining that some Australian soldiers had been drunk and swam naked in a public place. The ADF acted on the complaint and investigated the incident.)[90]

RAMSI's image as a capable force aiming to serve the population was carefully crafted even before the first contingent of soldiers and police stepped off the C-130 Hercules aircraft at Henderson Field. Nick Warner sent his public relations representative ahead of the contingent's arrival to gauge the most effective means of communicating with the public and to develop initial concepts for communicating RAMSI messages to its members.[91] The Big Three also decided on a campaign for shaping indigenous perceptions that would at once encourage the law-abiding citizen while causing others to think twice before continuing their criminal activities. Warner explained,

> The idea was to go in with an overwhelmingly large military force . . . so that the militants quickly came to the conclusion that it would be futile to resist. . . . We had the *Manoora* offshore. Now it's not a battleship, but it's pretty imposing with helicopters flying off it. . . . It wasn't meant to be in-your-face threatening, not in your face. It was background, meant to show this was serious. . . . Things we did on day one and the first month were all aimed at a public affairs impact. . . . We wanted to make a big footprint right away. . . . We wanted there to be joint patrols with the SI [Solomon Islands] police from day one. We wanted RAMSI personnel on key government buildings' security on day one. . . . I went and discussed this with the press. The audience was the population and the bad guys—and maybe there are three—the good guys in the government, too. . . . It was calculated and deliberately done.[92]

---

[90] European Centre on Pacific Issues (2003).

[91] Foster (2005).

[92] Warner (2005).

John Frewen provided the tactical perspective as well as insights regarding General Cosgrove's reasoning behind the soft but definitive demonstration of force:

> Shortly after dawn, the Hercs are landing, the *Manoora* appears off shore and the landing craft are coming ashore. Six or seven hours later, the commercial aircraft arrives and Nick Warner, Ben McDevitt, and [AusAID's] Margaret Thomas walk off the aircraft. [General Cosgrove had given me his guidance earlier. He said,] "This is going to set the tone for the Australian Army in the region for the next ten years. You are going to get off the aircraft without flak jackets, helmets, smiling and waving."[93]

The message was a carefully crafted one. RAMSI soldiers exited the aircraft prepared for resistance, but they "quickly sensed the mood and shouldered weapons to wave to elated crowds."[94] The Solomon Islanders who had been waiting for the planes waved to the arriving soldiers and police. Men, women, and children saw an armed and able but nonthreatening force. The message was one of comforting strength. It was otherwise for any in the population contemplating resistance. The *Minoora*'s appearance off shore just as the initial Hercules touched down at the airport was deliberately orchestrated. RAMSI was not only a large, very well-equipped force; it was one that could bring all its capabilities to bear with precise efficiency. The impressive demonstration of capability validated what Lt Col Luke Foster had been saying for weeks. That Ben McDevitt's police and John Frewen's soldiers were on the streets the same afternoon reinforced what their ears and eyes had been telling them: RAMSI meant business, and it wasn't business as usual.

There was no let-up on day two. Police patrols increased in number and expanded their coverage while backed by soldiers in an obviously supporting but nonetheless highly visible role. The Big Three immediately began taking their message to the people personally, explaining why RAMSI was in their country, what it would do for the population,

---

[93] Frewen (2005b).

[94] McDevitt (2005b).

what Solomon Islanders could do to assist in bringing about a better way of life, and willingly answering questions to address the inevitable misunderstandings and rumors that either inadvertently arose or were planted deliberately by foes of any counterinsurgency effort. Nick Warner explained,

> AusAID had contacted Kate Graham [a public affairs advisor] before we came out. She contracted for a weekly radio program called *Talking Truth*. . . . We used that program and used radio generally to get the message out. [We did not rely greatly on newspapers.] And it got to the point that we'd take *Talking Truth* with us, and sit down in a shack and have 100 to 150 people sitting around us ask us questions. "You're only here to take our logs . . . You're about to leave and we'll be subjected to these bad people." It was extremely important for the three of us to actually go out and have contact with the Solomon Islands people, to explain our objectives and reassure them of our commitment.[95]

RAMSI leaders attempted to control the environment and sustain the population's favorable perceptions well beyond initial impressions. CTF 635 commander Frewen's policy of avoiding the potentially negative impact of the large numbers of outsiders on the nation's economy was but a part of his and other leaders' vision. Frewen also "didn't want military vehicles driving in the streets. He didn't want soldiers walking around with guns [during their free time]. . . . You sort of had a silent hand. . . . It didn't interfere with the Solomon Islander's normal life."[96] The senior military commander drew on lessons from Australia's previous operations in designing these policies, recalling,

> Soldiers can rapidly disrupt the economy and eat out the warehouse, and that leads to resentment. I also didn't want troops sitting around in bars setting a bad example for the local youth. It was a non-liquor mission anyway, but still didn't want the bad example. . . . Where I put the headquarters and troops, the Gua-

---

[95] Warner (2005).

[96] Watson (2005b).

dalcanal Beach Resort, was pretty much out of the way and difficult to get to. [We heard of rumors that people thought it was] a secret base, that there was a large force at the Guadalcanal Beach Resort, and the population was convinced it was poised, ready to come out and pounce wherever it was needed.[97]

James Watson recalled the scene as he exited the plane on arriving. He looked out on those who had gathered for the event: "It was a sea of black faces. The people were smiling."[98] The leaders of RAMSI wanted to ensure that the people kept smiling.

The first of RAMSI's public open-house capability demonstrations took place only ten days after arrival. It was yet another means of reinforcing the message of friendly competence and latent capability. Soldiers from the five nations were

> doing the typical public relations stuff such as putting camouflage on kids' faces. It was a massive public relations coup. We had equipment displays, but most importantly we had dogs digging weapons out of the ground. We had mine detectors finding buried weapons. And we let people look through night-vision goggles. Rumors started that the dogs could pick a criminal out of the crowd. We had UAVS. "People thought they could see through roofs and find them hiding in their cupboards, that they could read people's minds and know they were having bad thoughts. [Word of mouth got] the message out. . . . The penalties for having a weapon were huge: $20,000 and ten years in jail. So people started turning in weapons and we started cutting them up in front of them."[99]

RAMSI representatives did not disabuse the population of its sometimes extraordinary beliefs in the force's capabilities, nor did they move to quash rumors supportive of the message RAMSI wanted to communicate to militia members or other potential threats. One

---

[97] Frewen (2005b).

[98] Watson (2005b).

[99] Frewen (2005b). Portions not in quotation marks are paraphrased.

member of the mission remembered that those helping with the open-day demonstrations were at times asked, "'Is it true that you can detect weapons in a house when you drive past?' We told them that we couldn't tell them about that. That we weren't at liberty to talk about whether we could see inside houses. . . . It wasn't a very technologically sophisticated culture, and it definitely helped with the weapons turn-in."[100]

The frequent patrolling and open days provided opportunities to interact with the locals, many of whom were young and ripe for influence by RAMSI members or less well-intentioned personalities with a little cash and an intent to use the youth for ill purposes, such as criminal activities. Police and soldiers alike capitalized on these opportunities, but here, too, mission leaders ensured that they maintained unity of message. Soldiers, regardless of their patrol route, carried cards that emphasized the one or two points currently most important to overall RAMSI objectives, the goal being consistency in public interactions throughout the islands. Messages were coordinated with the police so that military and law enforcement information was mutually supporting.[101] John Hutcheson found that Solomon Islanders were worried on hearing that the number of soldiers would be reduced as time passed. A daily message agreed to across all RAMSI agencies sought to mitigate these worries, reminding the population that the military had always played a supporting role. It was the police who had been guaranteeing their protection since day one of the undertaking. They would continue to do so regardless of the military's reductions in force.[102] RAMSI's willingness to back guarantees of security were repeatedly demonstrated to the public when soldiers were redeployed to the islands in the wake of police officer Dunning's murder, and again in May 2005 and April 2006 in response to increased instability, including the demonstrations during which Australian and local police were injured.[103]

---

[100]Anonymous interview.

[101]Hutcheson (2005b).

[102]Hutcheson (2005b).

[103]"In and Out Prime Minister" (2006); "Australian Reinforcements Land In Honiara" (2006); Kilcullen (2006b).

Police patrols were consistently a medium for communicating messages of every sort. From Ben McDevitt's ensuring that there was a patrol on the afternoon of the day of arrival to the above-mentioned reinforcement of police primacy, these ever ongoing, low-level tactical events reinforced the words spoken by the Big Three and helped to ensure that RAMSI's accomplishments were widely known. The police and soldiers—RAMSI personnel and Solomon Islander RSIP members alike—provided the voices that constantly reminded all: "Criminal activities will not be tolerated, and if there are criminal activities, this is the force that will be used."[104] It was RAMSI police, in partnership with their Solomon Islands counterparts, who encouraged parents to allow their children to return to school, an accomplishment achieved within two weeks of the coalition's arrival. Mark Bonser saw this as a significant measure of the operation's success; "Honiara was the first place [we focused on], and next was the Weather Coast. . . . The real sign to me that this was back under control was that school was open and all the children were back in school in the Weather Coast area."[105] The patrols were a constant reminder of the positive nature of RAMSI's efforts. While AusAID, NZAID, and other governmental and nongovernmental aid agencies provided assistance to islanders through projects large and small, soldiers and police on patrol further reinforced in peoples' minds the benefits that RAMSI brought to the country. Patrol members exchanged youths' offensive t-shirts and dirty camouflage clothing for clean, less belligerent wear. Patrols helped to identify what groups could benefit from the distribution of axes, saws, and other tools, and where aid station locations would be particularly helpful. These seemingly small acts were all part of the effort to shape public attitudes. Ben McDevitt called them "quick hits," actions that had an immediate yet memorable impact on those who benefited.[106] Patrols reinforced the unity-of-message campaign through words, actions, and simple reassuring presence, all of which were, in turn, reinforced by other RAMSI agencies.

---

[104]Bonser (2005).

[105]Bonser (2005).

[106]McDevitt (2005a).

The compactness of the RAMSI enterprise facilitated this unity of message. Nick Warner and his DFAT representatives acted as the clearinghouse for all media messages. This policy at times caused delays in releasing messages, something the national contingents other than the Australians at times found frustrating. It appears that such friction never became a major issue, however, certainly not one that endangered the consistency of communications made available to local and international audiences. Inordinate delays can undermine or destroy the effectiveness of shaping efforts. That the primary challenges confronted in the Solomon Islands were fairly uniform across the population was a significant factor in such centralization not having more negative consequences (despite the heterogeneity of subcultures and languages). One should also not underestimate the importance of the discipline in supporting the unity of message effort demonstrated by RAMSI participants.

The success of the shaping campaign and maintenance of unity of message was a further demonstration of how important interagency, multinational, and interdisciplinary cooperation is during counterinsurgency operations. Shaping—and the development of messages that support it—cannot succeed without accurate information and intelligence. Intelligence is never an end in itself. During counterinsurgency campaigns it serves not only to inform regarding the capabilities and intentions of adversaries, but also—and perhaps even more importantly—to educate with respect to the noncombatants whose support will ultimately determine the success or failure of the COIN effort. Quentin Flowers found this no less true during his tenure as second commander of CTF 635 than did John Frewen before him and those who followed in that position:

> Information Operations (including psychological operations and public affairs) were an essential ingredient to the success of this operation, particularly given the rumour-hungry nature of Melanesian society and the extensive social trauma that prevailed. From a military perspective, the widest possible popular visibility was essential for tactical overmatch to be an effective deterrence.

Audiences were identified, and products developed, through close liaison with local experts, trusted stakeholders and sample groups. . . . The quest for reliable "grass-roots" information was a constant and significant challenge through this operation. The rumour-hungry Melanesian culture, endemic corruption and traumatised and deprived population consistently produced agenda-driven information that frequently had little basis in fact. The most workable approach to sourcing reliable information, or verifying the reliability of information obtained, was through a combination of trusted and well-connected local personalities, frequent patrols and regular high level visits.[107]

Lest it be thought that RAMSI was unchallenged in its efforts to shape the Solomon Islands public, Peter Noble reminds us that many corrupt officials had little desire to see any real change in the nation's political processes. Some resisted RAMSI's initial arrival, as the status quo was filling their pockets.[108] For others, the coalition was seen as a means of neutralizing the militia factions that had become such a drain on government funds that there was insufficient money to support their own graft. Many in public positions welcomed RAMSI's efficiency in arresting Harold Keke and the improvement in the security situation as the precursors for a return to previous types of corruption. RAMSI leaders had to counter efforts to discredit the mission after its initial success, efforts gauged to force the mission's withdrawal. Nick Warner and his colleagues demonstrated significant wisdom in this regard by maintaining control of the lever most influential when dealing with those driven by greed. Speaking of those who sought RAMSI's early departure, an individual familiar with the political situation remembered,

> Their strategy, this is not a formal strategy . . . was to stonewall RAMSI . . . [to employ a] strategy of doing nothing and RAMSI would be discredited. . . . When the report [by other southwest Pacific nations' representatives] came in, it blamed the Solomon

---

[107] Flowers (2005, written comments).

[108] McDevitt (2005b).

Islands government, not RAMSI, for the problems. . . . They were trying to grab at anything to discredit RAMSI, like, "Why are your soldiers out with his daughter?" But once they realized we had control over the finances, they realized that the influence was with us.[109]

The successful shaping and unity of message demonstrate the value in minimizing the bureaucratic seams that can deny interagency, multinational, governmental, nongovernmental, and commercial coalition members the common understanding and shared purpose that are essential to favorably influencing COIN environments. That such stovepiping initially existed is evident in the above discussion of interagency operations. It is to the credit of the Big Three and other RAMSI leaders that they ceaselessly refused to allow such divisions to come between themselves, and that they both fought and encouraged their subordinates to fight the perpetuation of such counterproductive bureaucratic cancers. An enemy on the battlefield seeks to find and exploit the boundaries between units, knowing that those seams separate forces less familiar with each other, less likely to have shared intelligence, and less comfortable with each other's capabilities. The battlefields of counterinsurgency and stability operations are more often the human mind and social organizations than physical terrain. An intelligent enemy looks for junctions between motivations; it desires to capitalize on bureaucratic jealousies and assails those rifts to separate supposed allies and sow distrust in the population. An organization that tolerates such seams, or whose members put individual interests before those collective, aids and abets the very foes it must eventually defeat to be successful.

---

[109] Anonymous interview.

CHAPTER FIVE

RAMSI: Was It a Counterinsurgency?

The language of irregular warfare has become as elusive as the guerrillas themselves. "Revolution," "subversion," "guerrilla warfare," "partisan warfare," and "insurgency" are spoken of with little precision, as though they were synonymous.

—Thomas R. Mockaitis (1990)

Counterinsurgency is a strange and complicated beast, and even following the principles and imperatives does not guarantee success.

—Headquarters, U.S. Department of the Army, and Headquarters, U.S. Marine Corps (2006)

Insurgency: An organized movement seeking to replace or undermine all or part of the sovereignty of one or more constituted governments through the protracted use of subversion and armed conflict.

Counterinsurgency: An organized effort to preclude or defeat an insurgency.

Given the above definitions, proposed in Chapter Two, was the situation that plagued the Solomon Islands prior to the arrival of RAMSI an insurgency?

Further investigation of insurgencies' character is helpful here, but it is first necessary not to limit the analysis to episodes overtly labeled as insurgencies. Many of those who have participated in or against an insurgency and later written of the experience call the episode by various names. Conceptualizations of insurgency based on 20th-century conflict often describe them as having overlapping steps, stages, or phases. Students of insurgency, irregular warfare, unconventional warfare, guerrilla warfare, and other forms of conflict akin to these can find the abundance of terms confusing, and confusing they often are, with many of the terms overlapping others in total or in part. Mao Tse Tung wrote of "the three stages" of his protracted warfare: the strategic defensive, strategic stalemate, and strategic offensive.[1] Roger Trinquier, a French officer with experience in counterinsurgency operations in Algeria in the middle of the last century, described his experiences as a different form of conflict entirely:

> A new form of warfare has been born. Called at times either *sub-versive warfare or revolutionary warfare*, it differs fundamentally from the wars of the past in that victory is not expected from the clash of two armies on a field of battle. . . . Warfare is now an interlocking system of actions—political, economic, psychological, military—that aims at the *overthrow of the established authority in a country and its replacement by another regime*. . . . What we are involved in is *modern warfare*.[2]

General Rupert Smith goes a step further, arguing, "War no longer exists," at least not "war as a battle in a field between men and machinery, war as a massive deciding event in a dispute of international affairs. . . . We are now engaged, constantly and in many permutations, in *war amongst the people*."[3]

Insurgency falls within the bounds of the various types of conflict addressed by these writers. This is an important realization: Without it, the student of insurgency deprives himself or herself of valuable material. That thinking includes Mao's delineation of three stages of his pro-

---

[1]   Mao (1977, p. 189); Headquarters, U.S. Department of the Army, and Headquarters, U.S. Marine Corps (2006, p. 1-5).

[2]   Trinquier (1985, p. 6). Emphasis in original.

[3]   Smith (2005, p. 404). Emphasis in original.

tracted war. It encompasses a similar division in the North Vietnamese *dau tranh* strategy for uniting the northern and southern parts of what is now a single country.[4] The U.S. Army and Air Force's post–Cold War low-intensity conflict manual also cited three "classical phases of a mass-oriented insurgency" (Phase 1: latent and incipient, Phase 2: guerrilla warfare, and Phase 3: war of movement), further observing, "Any phase in a mass-oriented insurgency may extend over a long period of time. A successful insurgency may take decades to start, mature, and finally succeed."[5] The already cited CIA's *Guide to the Analysis of Insurgency* instead offers four stages:

> *Preinsurgency*—Leadership emerges in response to domestic grievances or outside influences;

> *Organizational*—Infrastructure built, guerrillas recruited and trained, supplies acquired, and domestic and international support sought;

> *Guerrilla warfare* —Hit-and-run tactics used to attack government. Extensive insurgent political activity—both domestic and international—may also occur simultaneously during this stage;

> *Mobile conventional warfare*—Larger units used in conventional warfare mode.[6]

John J. McCuen, author of *The Art of Counter-revolutionary War: The Strategy of Counter-insurgency*, published in 1966, similarly outlines four stages, though his first is "organization . . . in which solid, popular bases are established in the countryside." His following three reflect a Maoist influence: terrorism, guerrilla warfare, and mobile warfare.[7] The U.S. Army and Air Force's Field Manual 100-20/Air Force Publication 3-20 is less explicit, stating only that "successful insurgen-

---

4   Pike (1986, p. 223).

5   Headquarters, U.S. Department of the Army, and Headquarters, U.S. Air Force (1990).

6   As quoted in Hoffman (2004, p. 17). Emphasis in Hoffman.

7   McCuen (undated). See also McCuen (1966).

cies pass through common phases of development. Not all insurgencies experience every phase, and progression through all phases is certainly not a requirement for success."[8]

The number of phases is frankly of little importance in our analysis regarding the Solomon Islands. What is relevant is the nature of the earliest actions in those phases. In virtually every case, the initial events in the chronology of an insurgency involve conceptualizing a plan, recruiting personnel, and consolidating resources prior to exposing the fledgling entity to the dangers of the outside world. Those writing about COIN emphasize that this is the most favorable time to quash an insurgency: During these very first steps, it lacks strength and coherence and is thus most vulnerable. With the passage of time, it becomes more organized and capable, and it begins to assert its increasing potency; denying the insurgency success is more difficult the longer it matures. The challenge, of course, is to detect these very first actions, or, if they are detected, to recognize them as an embryonic insurgency.

Here again it is valuable to confront the realization that an insurgency can be more than a politically motivated strategy guided by a far-reaching vision and well-defined end state. Certainly, the writings of Mao and former North Vietnamese seek to portray such grand coherence. Yet just as "no plan survives contact with the enemy," surely no insurgency sticks unwaveringly to whatever strategy its leaders initially envisioned (if they in fact developed anything akin to a strategy). Persistence, drive, and, yes, luck will all play a role in the extent of the insurgency's success. There are surely brilliant strategies that have been seen through to fruition, albeit with adaptations along the way; perhaps Mao's and Lenin's qualify. There are equally likely instances of near-"accidental" insurgencies in which fortune presents what are little more than criminal groups or ill-organized dreamers with successes far beyond what logic would dictate as justly theirs. The situation in the Solomon Islands was between these extremes. Harold Keke and his followers in the Weathercoast region certainly lacked the acumen and resources of a Lenin, Mao, or Ho Chi Minh. Yet, they already

---

8   Headquarters, U.S. Department of the Army, and Headquarters, U.S. Air Force (1990).

controlled a portion of Guadalcanal, had eliminated any opponents sent to remove them as a threat, touted a cause, and possessed a leader capable of inspiring or intimidating sufficient numbers among the population to at least hold onto the areas gained, if not eventually expand their influence further. They also had been in close proximity to a very effective insurgency for a number of years—that of the Bougainville Revolutionary Army—and had been directly or indirectly affected by that insurgency and its aftermath, very possibly giving them an understanding of basic insurgency concepts.[9] One can only guess whether Keke had a realistic strategy for capitalizing on his strengths, but he was an authority in an environment lacking much in the way of coherent governance. His was a capability seemingly able to expand into the vacuum of legitimacy. The threat was sufficient enough to focus the attention of RAMSI's leaders and cause those in Honiara to dispatch efforts to eradicate him. It is impossible to firmly determine whether his or others of somewhat lesser capacity were insurgencies in very early form, but it would have been foolhardy to assume that no threat existed. The experts assert that the best time to defeat an insurgency is in its first phase, i.e., a point at which it is very difficult to determine whether it is, in fact, an insurgency. Those so interrupted are insurgencies that never were. The evidence points to the Solomon Islands being just such a case.

---

[9] Thanks to David Kilcullen for this observation regarding the likely influence of the Bougainville insurgency. Kilcullen (2006b).

CHAPTER SIX

Fitting the RAMSI Square Peg into the World's Round Holes

It is extremely difficult for an army which has so great a preoc-cupation with armoured and mechanized warfare to concentrate sufficiently on this subject, but as it is far more likely to crop up, and as action in the early stages of a counter-insurgency cam-paign may well condition events for years to come, it is of the greatest importance that all concerned have a clear understanding of the issues involved. At the moment they do not.

—Frank Kitson (1987)

Fifty percent of the population is women, and they are impor-tant sources of intelligence. . . . You tell an infantry patrol that a woman is going to come along and there's resistance [but] people tend to talk more readily to a woman, especially other women. Of course the willingness of men to talk to women depends on the culture. And use your coalition members. The PNG guys spoke the language, as did some from other islands. Put them in your patrols.

—Lieutenant Colonel John Hutcheson,
third CTF 635 commander (2005b)

Why *counterinsurgency in a test tube*? The RAMSI mission comes closer to completely controlling every aspect of a counterinsurgency opera-tion (or, arguably a stability operation) than any other in recent history. This remarkable accomplishment has come about in an operation with quite a limited number of military and police personnel and with a command structure in which armed forces personnel were subordinate to civil authorities at the tactical, operational, and strategic levels of war (though "levels of operation" or "levels of campaign" would be a more appropriate designation in the case of RAMSI). Further, no individual interviewed in support of this research ever cited "control" or "controlling the environment" as an overtly articulated goal, yet the actions taken and decisions made at each step of RAMSI's progress de facto served to support the maintenance of control over every relevant activity. The U.S. Army's overarching doctrine of the latter Cold War years cited "initiative" as one of four primary operational tenets.[1] Retaining the initiative is good; maintaining control is better. The latter inherently implies the former.

Of course, RAMSI is not a controlled experiment. It is hard enough to control conditions completely in a laboratory; it is impossible to do so in the field. That those involved in and supporting the mission so closely approximated control merits analysis of their achievement, what lessons it offers, and what the implications of those lessons are for other counterinsurgency challenges both present and future. That RAMSI was arguably an all too rare case of preemptive counterinsurgency further enhances the potential value of such an investigation. That the undertaking was initially a dramatic success as a stability operation and effort to assist an ailing government in reestablishing its capabilities is undeniable even in the absence of any insurgent threat.

Major Vern Bennett's observation that the Solomon Islands operation offers a model rather than a template is critical to any such investigation. Just as every operational lesson learned represents a square peg in a round hole world, so every historical event provides only a clay image for practitioners of the arts of war, diplomacy, or other form of conflict. One has to round the sharpness from the square peg's edges before trying to apply it to another contingency. Similarly, the artist must reshape the clay of historical teachings if they are to provide value when confronting later challenges. As effective as Gerald Templer's approach was in Malaya, as adept as the Big Three and their colleagues

---

[1]   See Headquarters, U.S. Department of the Army (1982, 1986). The four tenets of Air-Land Battle were initiative, agility, depth, and synchronization.

at every echelon in the Solomon Islands were, theirs are but rough models for students and practitioners contemplating other events at other times. The original practitioners understood that theirs had to be an ever-changing model, one reshaped again and again to adapt to a constantly evolving insurgency environment. Templer, Warner, McDevitt, Frewen, and their successors were always reshaping some part of operations with an eye to better meeting new conditions. Taking the model into a completely different environment demands much more dramatic modifications. It may well be that only its core characteristics survive, but those alone will provide considerable value.

The changes demanded in such a transition are unfortunately very complex. Applying insights gained from a study of RAMSI requires much more than simply multiplying assets some 200 times over to match force strengths or other conditions. There are in fact many reasons to argue for casting aside the Solomon Islands experience as irrelevant to current enterprises in Iraq or Afghanistan, or any of greater scale in future years. There is the "not invented here" syndrome, a refusal to accept the value of material because it is not of native origin. There are admittedly considerable differences in scale. There was the long-term presence in the Solomon Islands of organizations such as AusAID and NZAID that were so crucial to maintaining at least a semblance of support infrastructure prior to the arrival of RAMSI. And then there is perhaps the most obvious difference: threats confronted in other insurgencies often differ in many ways from the generally poorly disciplined, ill-supplied, and unpopular militias and gangs of Guadalcanal and Malaita. Surely, some will argue, that alone makes any consideration of this contingency one of doubtful value to Iraq, Afghanistan, and virtually anywhere else.

The threat admittedly received rather limited attention in previous pages. The threat was limited but not negligible. The Big Three agreed to the initial priorities of disarming the militias and capturing the most heinous of their leaders. Harold Keke's surrender was widely touted as the most important single event in the first 12 months of the operation. Potential force impressed upon militia, criminal, and innocent alike that resistance would be a futile endeavor; soldier readiness on disembarking aircraft and the initiation of patrols the very afternoon of their arrival combined with other deliberately evident signs demonstrating the capabilities that RAMSI could bring to bear. Yet the application of superior firepower and combat vehicles roaring through town and countryside were not part of that success. The military component was vital to the interagency, multinational, and shaping operations that served and continue to serve as the foundation for the mission's accomplishments. There are many threat-related "what ifs" that would have significantly altered the nature of progress toward those feats. What if Keke and the GLF had chosen to resist? What if the authorities from neighboring island nations had sided with corrupt politicians seeking RAMSI's ouster after the initial successes? What if one or more soldiers had mistakenly shot and killed an innocent civilian in the initial days, an enemy, perhaps, having deliberately baited the event? Certainly, the character of progress would have differed from that in actuality. The ultimate successes might have been delayed. But the long-term nature of the participants' commitment; their dedication to mission above individual, organizational, or national agendas; the striving for interagency and multinational compatibility; and adherence to a mission-wide unified message argue that RAMSI would nonetheless have succeeded. The threat should not be the primary focal point or center of gravity during a counterinsurgency operation. It is, rather, popular support—local and abroad—that is fundamental. Separating the population from the foe is crucial. Convincing the citizenry that their future is a brighter one if they support the friendly cause rather than the adversary propels every forward step. Successful models for Iraq, Afghanistan, and other contingencies will be very different from that for RAMSI, but there will be vital elements in common. The previous early success in East Timor offers further evidence that far more than good fortune underlies the achievements in the Solomon Islands.[2]

---

[2]   Kilcullen (2006b).

Vital Elements: Building on the Foundation of Successful Interagency, Multinational, and Shaping Operations

Four elements are common to the three foundational components of successful interagency, multinational, and shaping operations that proved so important to RAMSI and the welfare of the Solomon Islands population. History demonstrates that all will likely have greater or lesser application to other COIN undertakings.

Intelligence

Intelligence is vital to success during any COIN operation, yet no other factor seems to breed a similar degree of controversy. Intelligence was mainstream in the above discussions of interagency, multinational, and shaping operations. The military, police, and diplomatic components of RAMSI each had their own approach to intelligence. Only after considerable debate and the destruction of bureaucratic firewalls was it commonly understood that there were complementary benefits to be had by all through improved sharing. New Zealanders' frustrations at being denied access to selected information was noted previously. Exclusion of other participants' representatives from RAMSI headquarters intelligence sections also bred ill feelings. It is stating the obvious to note that successful shaping of indigenous attitudes is impossible without effective intelligence, as are effective psychological operations against a foe. The seams that interfered with successful exchanges during the first weeks of operations in the Solomon Islands have a long ancestry. Some British leaders in Iraq have been frustrated when they felt that their soldiers' lives were put at risk because of U.S. unwillingness to provide access to SIPRNET and intelligence materials. Interorganizational barriers meant that exchanges between the U.S. military, CIA, Army of the Republic of Vietnam, and other intelligence organizations were often handicapped or completely blocked during the war in Vietnam. The refusal to tolerate the maintenance of intelligence empires during RAMSI helped to tear down similar impediments. That RAMSI forces had asserted themselves immediately on arrival in theater points to a need to solve intelligence problems before, rather than after, deployment. Collocation during planning and operations will help to block their construction, as will strong leadership intolerant of bureaucratic excuses.

Leadership

A second common element of success is the importance of selecting the right person for the job. The ability and dedication to a common cause demonstrated by the Big Three was a frequent theme throughout this study, one that permeated every aspect of RAMSI operations. Less obvious, perhaps, was the vital importance of the squad leader who restrained his impulse to interfere with police work, or the law enforcement officers who avoided the temptations of graft, instead maintaining an unbroken commitment to a population motivated to once again trust their police. A lapse at any one of the several remote police outposts throughout the islands could have seriously undermined the operation's legitimacy. The personal involvement of Nick Warner and Ben McDevitt in the opening of those stations surely communicated the importance of operations there to those staffing them, as well as to the local population each served. Ultimately, however, the restraint and professionalism demonstrated many miles from Honiara underpinned the long-term objective of convincing citizens that perhaps the police could once again be trusted. General Cosgrove understood the importance of the individual in a world in which a single incident can bolster or threaten the success of an entire mission:

> In my day, as a junior leader, my decisions had an immediate impact on my troops and the enemy. In today's military operations the decisions of junior leaders still have those immediate impacts, but modern telecommunications can also magnify every incident, put every incident under a media microscope, and send descriptions and images of every incident instantly around the world for scores of experts and commentators to interpret for millions of viewers and listeners. Thus the decisions of junior leaders and the actions of their small teams can influence the course of international affairs.[3]

---

[3]   Ryan (2000, p. 72).

Sometimes the crucial leadership involves the supervision of thousands. In other instances, it may apply to less than a handful or manifest as self-control. Americans deployed to Afghanistan and Iraq have described incidents in which newly arrived units expressed—verbally or through their actions—aggressiveness unsuited to their counterinsurgency responsibilities. They come with a desire to demonstrate a warrior's acumen, a proof of heroism marked by engaging an enemy or earning combat medals. The mindset is obviously problematic when restraint rather than belligerence is called for. Such concerns are not limited to the U.S. military. A quote from Peter Londey on page 8 in Chapter One highlighted New Zealand's concerns with Australians' aggressive posture in East Timor. Australians themselves also had apprehensions in this regard, despite the commendable self-discipline shown by their personnel during RAMSI. Lt Col John Hutcheson, when asked what he would have sought to introduce in preparing others for future Solomon Islands rotations, cited

> the application of force at all critical levels. It is important to understand the difference between the Arnold Schwarzenegger–type soldier and the soldier there to keep the peace. A soldier in a helmet, flak vest, and wearing wrap-around sunglasses is more likely to disquiet those who see him—or see an image of him in the media—than reassure that he is there to keep the peace. One component of approaching such situations effectively is to develop leaders at all levels who understand ethically what is right and wrong. A second is to *ensure those leaders know how to apply force to achieve desired outcomes.*[4]

Other forms of restraint were no less important to the early successes during RAMSI. Individual and organizational agendas were virtually invisible at the mission's upper-leadership echelons. Harold Keke's surrender is an apt example. Perhaps naïve in his way, Keke

---

[4] Hutcheson (2005b, 2006). Note that Lieutenant Colonel Hutcheson's comment regarding leaders and the use of force implies knowing the extent to which force, the threat of force, or other approaches in lieu of those involving force are appropriate given a specific situation.

was nevertheless an able leader and a formidable foe. His influence in causing the successive surrender of so many of his followers and their laying down of arms exemplifies that status. It is further evident in Ben McDevitt's recollection of the surrender event: "Keke's profound influence upon his people was such that as he said his goodbyes to the hundreds of followers who were on the beach at Mbiti, many of them were in tears and visibly distressed. Many of these people had seen Keke as their protector and believed that once he was gone they would fall prey to other warlords who had also been terrorizing the Weathercoast."[5] Both McDevitt's negotiation skills and the trust built between Nick Warner and Keke were elementary to the outcome. The individual talents were key to the success, but it was their unified coalition that left the foe without any apparent alternative. Keke had no seam to exploit. Police, military, and diplomatic suasion were united. International representatives provided a solid front. Individual skills influenced Keke's decision to surrender, the coalition's unanimity constantly serving to reinforce his perception that no other course of action offered a reasonable prospect of success.

The positive impact of RAMSI's leadership would be hard to overstate. It would be misleading to limit the observation to those on the islands alone, however. The trust given to them and the freedom of action that accompanied that trust meant that the Big Three unceasingly retained the means essential to the control of their environment. The unified front presented by the RAMSI leadership to Canberra and other nations' capitals surely played an important role in maintaining this freedom of action, but the original choice of leaders and the independence provided them minimized inconsistencies in policy that sow doubt in the minds of an indigenous population and provide hope to an enemy. Unfailing commitment to the long term, RAMSI's consistent oversight of how funds were used, and maintenance of public support via the exercise of restraint in the use of force all meant that the seams a militia leader or corrupt Solomon Island politician might seek to exploit were few in number and limited in size. RAMSI leaders' control of the purse strings was particularly important in this regard. They

---

5   McDevitt (2005b).

determined who received aid; their orders influenced who was investigated for corruption. Equally important: Their decisions were not
overturned by political leaders within or beyond the Solomon Islands.
Unity of message was maintained in Australian Prime Minister John
Howard's declarations of intent to stay the course and in the daily
messages communicated by police and soldiers on patrol. The messages, from on high or via the street, were kept simple and thus as free
of misinterpretation or deliberate misconstruing as possible. Innocent
and enemy alike saw leadership unified horizontally across national
and interagency boundaries and vertically from the highest to lowest
levels of authority.

Control

It is also important to note the care taken to immediately establish
the legitimacy of indigenous Solomon Islands government authorities
while RAMSI also retained the control necessary to bring about the
reforms vital to long-term success. RAMSI leaders had to constantly
shield the mission from corrupt officials' efforts to undermine its legitimacy. That the mission came to the Solomon Islands at the request of
the nation's executive and legislative leaders was essential, as was the
relief of its members from prosecution under local law (which could
have entangled them in arrests or lawsuits motivated by local officials'
political agendas). While the Solomon Islands government must renew
the RAMSI charter annually, the continued support of key political
leaders (most notably the prime minister) and among the local population sustains confidence that the long-term commitment will not be
threatened from the islands themselves. (It helps that economic growth
and other improvements have accompanied the successes in the security
situation. The Solomon Islands government had a 40-percent increase
in revenues in 2004.)[6] That RAMSI owed its presence to the government of Prime Minister Sir Alan Kemakeza and the country's parliament, and that mission members worked closely alongside government
officials rather than replacing them, meant that residents were always
governed by their own leaders while mission personnel assumed the

---

[6] Downer (2005).

roles of advisors and providers of assistance rather than occupiers. Solomon Islanders were made part of patrols from day one, even though RAMSI police and soldiers both had full arrest authority. That applied for all ten nations' police representatives regardless of position; Ben McDevitt served as a member of the RSIP in his role as deputy commissioner of that force, not as an authority external to the law enforcement system. RAMSI did not replace the rule of law with one of its own making; it returned to that existent before societal breakdown. That is not to say that the mission avoided change. Social engineering was on the agenda; corruption would not be tolerated regardless of its prevalence and spread. While RAMSI introduced what some might consider Western—and therefore foreign—standards of political responsibility, the changes were undertaken without extralegal activities or violation of Solomon Islands cultural norms. The population recognized that it would benefit from the changes being imposed; it unsurprisingly supported such engineering. RAMSI thereby secured a vital precondition for success: the authority necessary to remove the cancer that otherwise would prevent a Solomon Islands recovery. It refused to surrender too easily the control essential to achieving the desired end while limiting its influence only to the extent necessary to achieve that end. These two elements–sufficient control and restraint–are arguably elemental to success in COIN scenarios involving in-place governments of marginal legitimacy. Embarking on a counterinsurgency effort without the authority and capability to remove those whose presence will inherently threaten an advantageous outcome is a dubious undertaking. The lessons of South Vietnam are but one example. Jeffrey Race echoes South Vietnamese citizens' frustration with local government officials (and misguided U.S. relief efforts), evidenced in the his classic *War Comes to Long An*:

> Looking back on the government assistance programs . . . Duoc considered the results were limited, and for three reasons: First and foremost, we must admit that the cadres were corrupt. If ten bags of cement were given out in Saigon, only one or two would actually be distributed. . . . Third, it was often inappropriate. For example, Vietnamese people like to eats rice, but we sent barley. Another example–mechanical plows are good for plowing dry

soil, but they don't work in marshy fields. Rather than supplying mechanical plows, it would have been better to supply a good buffalo-drawn plow and some water buffalo.[7]

Both aspects of Race's observation provide lessons for those undertaking COIN. RAMSI leaders kept control of the ultimate lever in a government reliant on graft: its funds. They also sought to ensure that those abusing the system most heinously were removed while others with promise were given the opportunity to change their ways. The activities critical to this rebuilding of a legitimate government were always ongoing. Although stability and security concerns dominated RAMSI's initial priority list, aid was never nonexistent. As the security situation improved, the mission executed a smooth and effective transition, increasing emphasis on aid, eradicating corruption, and bolstering Solomon Islanders' self-sufficiency. It is important to have such a comprehensive approach, one that includes the appropriate and early staffing of indigenous government agencies with coalition personnel able to at once oversee operations and conduct on-the-job training for their indigenous counterparts. Mark Etherington served as Iraq's Coalition Provisional Authority (CPA) senior representative in Al Kut in 2003 and 2004. He reminds us that money alone is insufficient when seeking to assist a nation's recovery. Addressing the inflow of CPA money to create a police force for the city, Etherington concluded, "It was clear that one might as well simply burn a million dollars as buy equipment for the police in their present state. It was hard to imagine a body of men less viable for law enforcement."[8] He went on to describe the virtual anarchy that existed as the CPA (perhaps too quickly) surrendered its authority to an indigenous Iraqi government, a transition that made removing corrupt officials impossible:

> Despite our dismissal of the former Chief of Police and his Deputy and the compelling reasons for it, our difficulties in confirming their successors officially at the Ministry of the Interior vividly

---

[7] Race (1972, p. 61).

[8] Etherington (2005, p. 61).

illustrated the internecine political tensions of the period. We had installed them in early April, and exhaustively explained why we had done so to the CPA and the Ministry. They had begun, with our encouragement, weeding out the weak and corrupt from a grotesquely swollen force, of whom only a minority ever reported for duty. After initial review they recommended the dismissal of fifty-five officers and men. Timm [Timothy Timmons, Etherington's American deputy] showed me two intercepted documents. The first, dated 4th May and signed by a Deputy Minister of the Interior, told the new Chief, Abdul Haneen . . . that he was "not to obey the orders of the British coordinator." The Ministry refused to confirm the new Chief and Deputy in post, and said that their attempts to reform the force must stop; indeed that only the Ministry could initiate such steps.[9]

The international Pacific Islands Forum Eminent Persons Group reminds us that quality, not speed, is the preferred measure of effectiveness. It is wisdom that should influence both the duration of any mission's commitment and rapidity with which local authorities are permitted to assume unsupervised control: "The tenure of RAMSI should be measured by the achievement of tasks rather than be time bound."[10] Andrew Alderson made a similar observation while serving as an economic planning and development advisor in Al Basrah, Iraq, in 2003–2004: "I believe that CPA made one fatal mistake. They are driven by an end date instead of an end state."[11]

Focus on the People

The Big Three and their subordinates never lost sight of their primary concern despite early priorities of disarmament and militia leader arrest: the welfare of the Solomon Islands citizenry and the essential support they offered the mission. Warner, McDevitt, and Frewen (or Frewen's successors after his departure) traveled to the troubled Weathercoast no

---

[9]   Etherington (2005, pp. 225–226).

[10]   "Mission Helpem Fred: A Review of the Regional Assistance Mission to Solomon Islands" (2005, p. 25).

[11]   Alderson (2004).

fewer than 50 times during the first year.[12] Such travel, the emphasis on daily patrol messages, and holding of open days and special events, such as Honiara cleanup day or "March for Peace Day" to celebrate the end of the gun amnesty period, regularly reinforced the value that RAMSI brought to the islands and the benefits that lay ahead. (See Figure 5.1.) True, the people were "on side" from the first moment of arrival, but none in RAMSI took the support for granted. There was no end to the honeymoon period because the good will was never permitted to lapse. The result was a continually supportive population, one whose faith and confidence in the foreigners and their promises increased as time passed. They did not turn against RAMSI as seeming occupiers. They increasingly become providers of intelligence as that confidence grew. They became a collective mouthpiece that further disseminated mission members' messages. That the messages came from fellow islanders made them all the more effective; it is a marketing truth that information passed on by familiar persons carries weight far greater than that from a less trusted source. It is also notable that RAMSI consistently delivered on promises made, a function of both the "whole of government" approach and the coordination-backing efforts to maintain unity of message.

This focus on the people reinforced police and soldiers' perceptions that the citizenry was largely friendly rather than an ever-present threat. There were no inadvertent deaths at roadblocks, no firing of rounds across the hoods of vehicles that approached too closely (a tactic practiced in Iraq, but one of dubious value in dissuading a driver with ill intentions). Restraint rather than quick trigger fingers characterized interactions with the population, Australian and ally alike. Experiences in Bougainville and East Timor had demonstrated that stability operations held their dangers, yet men and women demonstrated patient good judgment even under conditions that permitted engagement. They thereby provided few opportunities for Solomon Islanders to desire vengeance.

---

[12] McDevitt (2005a).

Figure 6.1
**Celebrating the End of Gun Amnesty on "March for Peace Day" in the
Solomon Islands**

SOURCE: Provided to the author by Ben McDevitt. Reprinted courtesy of the
Government of Australia, Department of Defence.
RAND MG551-6.1

Implications for Current and Future Operations

Interagency Operation Considerations

Interagency coordination during operations in Iraq was not what it
should have been. Below is but one example, one hard to conceive of
in the Solomon Islands given the close relationship maintained by the
RAMSI Big Three, and certainly not nearly a year after initiation of
operations:

> The disparity in processes and procedures was highlighted when
> CPA developed and planned to announce a new policy to improve
> the security of Iraqi borders. On 2 March 2004, simultaneous

bombing attacks in Karbala and Baghdad killed more than 150 Shiite worshippers during festivals to observe Ashura. . . . Within hours of the attacks, the CPA Senior Advisor to the Ministry of the Interior established a working group to develop specific actions that could be quickly implemented and announced. Two days after the Ashura bombings, the working group had produced a short memo of recommendations that was provided to Ambassador Bremer, who handed a copy to the CJTF-7 [Coalition Joint Task Force 7] Commander, Lieutenant General [Ricardo] Sanchez. The memo included a handful of actions that would be requested of CJTF-7 in support of the new policy.

This was the first time that Lieutenant General Sanchez had seen the proposed policy. From the CJTF-7 point of view, this was a significant staffing failure. It turned out that the CPA working group either simply forgot to invite CJTF-7 to participate or viewed the development of border security policy as an issue with little relevance to CJTF-7 because most of the proposals were specific to CPA or the Iraqi Ministry of the Interior, with only a minor support role suggested for CJTF-7. Furthermore, the CPA staff saw nothing wrong with Lieutenant General Sanchez being the first person in CJTF-7 to see the policy.[13]

One must be careful not to criticize too quickly, nor should one too readily accept excuses for inaction. RAMSI participants themselves questioned whether meeting daily and whether the level of personal interaction maintained by the Big Three would have been possible were conditions different. Perhaps not, but that does not diminish the importance of major leaders' frequent coordination and diligence in ensuring that their colleagues in other agencies are well and frequently informed. Collocation of key personalities and staff sections, appointment of able and qualified liaison officers in sufficient numbers, and intolerance of personal and bureaucratic agendas are all hallmarks of RAMSI success that offer lessons for operations in Iraq and elsewhere, and that cannot be justifiably cast aside because of differences in scope or size. The existence of a single point of contact in Canberra through

---

[13] Schnaubelt (2005–2006, p. 54).

which all issues were routed ensured that those on the ground in the Solomon Islands had a champion in the hallways of the lead nation's capital. Misunderstandings regarding various agency planning methods or staff procedures hindered RAMSI, but agencies adapted and now seek to institute academic and operational exchanges of personnel to reduce the likelihood of such issues during future RAMSI rotations or other operations. U.S. Department of Defense schools and doctrine writers are incorporating lessons from Afghanistan and Iraq into curricula and manuals quicker and more effectively than ever in history. There has been notably less progress in advancing interagency coordination and understanding.

Multinational Operation Considerations

The RAMSI approach to multinational operations similarly offers fodder for improvement. Police and military personnel alike found many familiar faces among those from other nations as they prepared to deploy. That is in part explained by the number of recent regional operations in the southwest Pacific, but it is also reflective of the commitment to developing professional exchanges that later provided such payoff. Similar U.S. exchanges should favor those nations with which it is most likely to work in future coalitions rather than traditional relationships more reflective of the Cold War era than of current operations. (The two are not always mutually exclusive, the relationship with the United Kingdom, Australia, and New Zealand being prime examples.) Personnel records should identify those who shared seminars with or sponsored international representatives (U.S. personnel tours with other nations' militaries are already so noted), and commanders should not be shy about asking allies for individuals by name when it comes to filling sensitive positions, training or operational, during deployments. They do so regularly within their own services; doing so with foreigners who have established professional reputations seems a natural extension.[14] The United States should be willing to reciprocate in cases in which friends in need request assistance from

---

[14] Requests for specific U.S. individuals to serve with other nations' militaries, and vice versa, do occur occasionally, but the instances are rare.

Americans with whom they are familiar. Exchanges need not be only with close allies. Australia's relationship with Indonesia is one rife with challenges. The behavior of the latter nation's army during operations in East Timor is but one example of recent misdeeds. Yet Australian-Indonesian exchanges continue unabated, and relationships developed as a result have often served both nations well. The tradition of maintaining military relationships even during difficult times dates to the 1960s, when Australia maintained diplomatic relations with Indonesia and continued to train Indonesian personnel at its jungle school in Canungra, even while engaging in combat operations against them during the Borneo Confrontation.[15]

The presumption that each nation be assigned its own area of responsibility also merits reconsideration. Wartime commanders have often intermixed veteran units with those newly arriving to stiffen the less experienced. Mission objectives might at times be better served were a similar approach taken when incorporating representatives in a multinational coalition. There are professional militaries whose commanders are perfectly capable of managing U.S. or any other nations' forces. There are organizations, military and otherwise, that lack the resources, training, or experience to lead at any but the lower tactical levels. Recent action in Iraq has demonstrated both situations; it would be wise to reassess what have become virtual standard procedures within coalition operations.

Leadership Considerations

The importance of RAMSI's leadership permeates every aspect of the discussions presented in this chapter. The cooperation demonstrated by the Big Three was exceptional. That talents matched demands was no less important. All obviously drew on previous experiences, and Australia, New Zealand, and other participating nations were fortunate in having had so broad a spectrum of contingencies to which leaders and subordinates alike had been exposed in recent years.

The United States has had a somewhat similar range of experiences. Unfortunately, a move toward emphasizing them in training

---

[15] Kilcullen (2006b).

has been somewhat slow. Only recently have training centers begun to move away from a primary emphasis on gunnery, combat reconnaissance, and force-on-force scenarios. Leader training at every echelon still spends far less time on governing issues and the types of challenges confronted daily in Afghanistan and Iraq than it does on wartime planning and execution. Scenarios in which the military is subordinate to another agency, as was the case with the police and army during RAMSI operations, are virtually unheard of, as are those in which another service assumes the army's traditional role as the supported arm.

The personalities of the Big Three and other leaders above and below them also merit notice. Major operations tend to be the realm of assertive personalities and active egos. Restraint rather than aggressiveness better describes the approach of the Big Three. Trust and a hands-off style similarly characterized the leadership of coalition political leaders at home when it came to dealing with those deployed. Lower-level leaders in the Solomon Islands reined in their aggressive tendencies; they exercised patience without dulling the sharpness of their units' performance. Governmental aid representatives stayed the course during even the worst of the violence, then integrated themselves into the frequent meetings chaired by the Big Three—the better to orchestrate RAMSI's diplomatic, police, military, and aid capabilities. That unity of message and effort has continued despite the transition from a mission dominated by security concerns to an aid-centric one speaks to the common dedication of leaders from all of these functional areas. That much of the day-to-day management fell to those in positions with a lower profile is evident in John Frewen's observation that "being a RAMSI principal took up about 70 percent of my time. . . . That left about 20 percent of my time trying to turn my headquarters into an efficient headquarters, and 10 percent of my time to go around and see the troops."[16] In short, Frewen had to leave much of the operational decisionmaking to trusted subordinates. The international character of agency staffs and leadership helped to ensure both that country interests were not overlooked and that sensitivities could

---

[16] Frewen (2005b).

be handled diplomatically. New Zealand's Major Vern Bennett, John Frewen's 2IC (equivalent to an executive officer in the U.S. military) not surprisingly found that his international status abetted perceptions of his impartiality when dealing with the occasional disagreement involving other than his own country's organizations.

The observations regarding aggressiveness beg the question of whether the same qualities of leadership so appreciated in combat are best suited for counterinsurgency operations in which an enemy is of secondary rather than primary importance. There are men and women whose abilities permit them to excel across much of the spectrum of conflict; there are others more able in some areas than others. Lt Col Jim Bryant conducted an analysis of RAMSI's early months. His perspective on the mission's leadership provides insights into the workings of its decisionmaking processes and the role of personality:

> Paul Symon is coordinating. He's meeting with Warner everyday and briefing him on what he needs to consider. . . . I think Frewen, Warner, Symon, and McDevitt are all good decision-makers. They aren't the typical Type A types. Warner is a great mind, but a great mind in the queen bee sense. And Symon knows how to communicate Warner's decisions to the military. . . . Everyone meeting nicely every morning. There's one boss, and it's Warner. There's no CFLCC [Coalition Forces Land Component Command], ORHA [Office of Reconstruction and Humanitarian Assistance], CPA.[17]

The consequences of choosing the right leader (or more importantly, building the right leadership team) are far too significant to leave to serendipity or permit selections based on talents better suited for other fields and challenges.

One other leadership element stands out as truly exceptional by U.S. standards. Peter Cosgrove's insistence on a single senior officer was simply recognition that "unity of command" is a desirable state of affairs during any military operation. That he put such trust in one of such junior rank is what distinguishes the choice. John Frewen com-

---

[17] Bryant (2005b).

manded a force of 1,800 men and women (300 of whom were from multinational partner militaries), some two to three times the size of a command normally given a lieutenant colonel. Further surprising is that Frewen does not appear to have been handpicked for the assignment. His was the command in "alert status" for the ADF at the time of the decision to deploy, and Cosgrove did not choose to interfere with the natural course of events. (However, the Chief of Defence Force was not unfamiliar with Frewen's abilities and character. Frewen worked as a captain for then-Colonel Cosgrove when the two were assigned to the Australian Army's Infantry Centre years before. Additionally, all Australian Army unit commanders are personally selected by the Chief of Army, the position held by General Cosgrove during the time of Lieutenant Colonel Frewen's selection for battalion command.)[18] Cosgrove's staying the course gave RAMSI the military leadership and modesty needed to meet its objectives during the crucial early months.

Final Observations on the Implications of RAMSI Operations for Counterinsurgency Operations

Nick Warner attributed RAMSI's first-year success in part to luck. Napoleon understood the value of luck, requiring but one quality in his marshals: "that they be lucky." It would be easy to cast aside the success of RAMSI as too small to be of value to larger contingencies, too unique for broader application, or simply the result of luck. Such an attitude would not merely be foregoing opportunity. It would also demonstrate a lack of appreciation for Australia's dedication to improving its operations. Clausewitz reminds us that "war is the realm of chance" (as are, by extension, other forms of human conflict).[19] True, but chance and luck favor those best prepared and most able. Previous successes elsewhere point to luck's fertile ground in which to take root prior to RAMSI's deployment.

---

[18] Kilcullen (2006b).

[19] Clausewitz (1976, p. 101).

In an early review of this study, New Zealand's Marion Craw-shaw reminded me that "it is too early to claim success." She is correct. Crawshaw recognizes the "huge success in terms of the objectives of the first year," but she reminds us that "enduring success will only start to be apparent a couple of years from now."[20] Her comment highlights the significance of a long-term commitment. It also emphasizes the impor-tance of not resting on past laurels. As is the case with any operation, the challenges in the Solomon Islands are evolving constantly. RAMSI must therefore evolve as well. The early success in improving the Sol-omon Islands' security and stability means that priorities have been revised. There is now more relative emphasis on capacity-building and assisting with the development of viable governmental structures. The real value of past successes is in setting the conditions to achieve these now more prominent objectives. The mission's organizational struc-ture and the roles of various agencies' leaders must be adapted to best meet these new demands. There can be no lessening of commitment, no reduction in intensity when planning and coordinating operations, no slackening in the quality of leadership. The interagency cooperation, orchestration of multinational talents, and maintenance of unity of message that were so important in those first years are equally impor-tant now. They will remain so during the years of commitment that lie ahead. Diligence in selecting the right personnel for deployment and appointing others who support RAMSI within participating nations' governments is as vital now as it was in mid-2003. History will judge RAMSI on its ultimate outcome, not its early successes. The wisdom behind Japanese warriors' advice to tighten one's helmet straps after initial success in battle applies no less to those conducting counter-insurgency operations and activities in their aftermath: Remain ever ready for action, for the greatest challenges may well lie ahead.

Fortunately, RAMSI has thus far been successful. The reasons for this offer lessons both for those committed to its future rotations and others undertaking COIN operations worldwide. It is said that success has many fathers. Certainly, the success of RAMSI is com-prised of many components: well-considered interagency coordination,

---

[20] Crawshaw (2006a).

multinational cooperation, fine leadership, disciplined and committed troops—the list is a lengthy one. The ancestry of RAMSI's success is equally extensive, influenced by Cambodia, Rwanda, Somalia, Afghanistan, Bougainville, East Timor, Iraq, and other missions worldwide. Those earlier contingencies also gave birth to an operational notion crafted for what the Australians and their allies have come to understand is a form of conflict that requires a different approach than does force-on-force combat (or "joint land maneuver" [JLM] in the parlance of Australian doctrine). The Australian Army has been working on its "control operations" concept for the better part of a decade. It is an initiative with roots in an investigation of urban warfare, but one that has rightly expanded to include a larger palette of challenges. The characteristics of JLM and its relationship to control operations are clear in the JLM definition:

> JLM operations are adversary centric, military-led operations in the land environment, supported by highly responsive joint effects, against an organized enemy, with the aim of setting conditions for effective control operations. JLM may precede, enable, or result from control operations.[21]

JLM differ from control operations in several fundamental ways. Joint Land Maneuver is

- adversary-centric
- military-led
- joint
- has an aim of defeating or destroying enemy combat element to set conditions.

Control operations, in contrast, are

- system-centric
- politically led
- interagency

---

[21] Freeman (2005).

- have an aim of dominating the overall environment to set conditions for nonmilitary agencies to return the society to normalcy.[22]

The definition of control operations incorporates these key elements:

> Control Operations are systems centric, interagency-led operations, in which land forces provide responsive support to interagency effects, against a diverse set of irregular adversaries. The aim is to dominate the overall environment in order to set conditions for other agencies to return the Area of Operations to normalcy.[23]

It is obvious that RAMSI falls within the purview of control operations. Unsurprisingly, the fit is not exact: The Solomon Islands mission was also joint in character, meaning that multiple military services participated rather than land forces alone. The important point, however, is that the defining character of RAMSI's success—control of virtually every aspect of the operational environment—cannot be attributed to luck, a serendipitous team of excellent leaders and personnel, or some other stroke of fate or fortune. Gaining and maintaining control was the result of a calculated and deliberately orchestrated effort. The many factors discussed at length above, and surely others as well, are all more or less key components of the effort; no invisible hand is responsible for the domination that set the conditions for success.

Also interesting is the extent to which operations in the Solomon Islands have been in accordance with historical and doctrinal observations regarding counterinsurgency operations. Below is a list of U.S. COIN historical principles, American COIN imperatives, and the British Army's counterinsurgency principles. Reading them in light of the lengthy discussions earlier in this chapter is sufficient to make clear how much RAMSI operations have in common with all three. The commonality is especially notable given that its executors did

---

[22] Freeman (2005).

[23] Freeman (2005).

not contemplate the undertaking as one involving counterinsurgency challenges.

U.S. Counterinsurgency Historical Principles

- "Legitimacy as the Main Objective"
- "Unity of Effort"
- "Political Primacy"
- "Understanding the Environment"
- "Intelligence as the Driver for Operations"
- "Isolation of Insurgents from their Cause and Support"
- "Security Under the Rule of Law."[24]

U.S. Contemporary Imperatives of Counterinsurgency

- "Manage Information and Expectations"
- "Use Measured Force"
- "Learn and Adapt"
- "Empower the Lowest Levels"
- "Support the Host Nation."[25]

British Army Principles of COIN

- "Ensure political primacy and political aim."
- "Build coordinated government machinery."
- "Develop Intelligence and Information."
- "Separate the insurgent from his support."
- "Neutralize the insurgent."
- "Plan for the long term."[26]

---

[24] Headquarters, U.S. Department of the Army, and Headquarters, U.S. Marine Corps (2006, p. 1-11–1-12).

[25] Headquarters, U.S. Department of the Army, and Headquarters, U.S. Marine Corps (2006, p. 1-13–1-14).

[26] British Army (2005 pp. 18–19).

The opening sentences of this chapter noted that the control attained was imperfect. Were RAMSI an experiment, it would be a flawed one. There were frictions between agencies and nations. Soldiers were not perfectly disciplined. A policeman was murdered; an Australian soldier would later die in an accident. But RAMSI wasn't an experiment. It was a real-world operation, exposed to human ill intentions, shortcomings, and fate's ever-wavering favor. That control was so effective offers lessons for leaders conducting other operations, those ongoing and ones yet to come. Conditions will differ; an equivalent degree of control could never have been attained in Iraq or Afghanistan. Yet the foundation lying beneath the control—well-executed interagency, multinational, and shaping operations—and the components that went into the building of a successful mission atop that foundation do apply to Iraq, Afghanistan, and future counterinsurgency challenges. Perfect control of all environmental conditions is impossible to attain on contested fields. Yet it is a worthy goal to pursue. As RAMSI demonstrates, success does not demand perfection.

Bibliography

Abuza, Zachary, "Alternate Futures for Thailand's Insurgency," *Terrorism Focus*, Vol. 3, No. 3, January 25, 2006, pp. 5–7. As of September 13, 2006:
http://www.jamestown.org/terrorism/news/uploads/tf_003_003.pdf

Alderson, Andrew, interview with Russell W. Glenn and Todd C. Helmus, Al Basrah, Iraq, February 23, 2004.

Alywin-Foster, Nigel, "Changing the Army for Counterinsurgency Operations," *Military Review*, November–December 2005, pp. 2–15. As of January 10, 2006:
http://usacac.army.mil/CAC/milreview/download/English/NovDec05/aylwin.pdf

Anzu, Bustin, "Maiden Journey into Provincial Policing," *AFPNews*, October 2005, pp. 13–14.

Assessing Community Perspectives in Governance in the Pacific, Foundation of the Peoples of the South Pacific International, October 31, 2003. As of September 17, 2006:
http://www.fspi.org.fj/program/governance/pdfs/
1%20RETA%206065%20(Regional).pdf

Australian Agency for International Development, *Annual Report 2003–2004*, Canberra, Australia, 2004. As of July 18, 2006:
http://www.ausaid.gov.au/anrep04/default.cfm

———, *Solomon Islands Transitional Country Strategy 2006 to mid-2007*, Canberra, Australia, March 2006a. As of September 13, 2006:
http://www.ausaid.gov.au/publications/pdf/solomons06_07.pdf

———, "Overseas Aid: Solomon Islands," May 2006b. As of September 13, 2006:
http://www.ausaid.gov.au/country/country.
cfm?CountryID=16&Region=SouthAsia

Australian Department of Foreign Affairs and Trade, "Arrest of Andrew Te'e," media release, December 8, 2003. As of September 17, 2006:
http://www.dfat.gov.au/media/releases/department/ramsi_031208.html

———, "Solomon Islands Country Brief," August 2006. As of September 13, 2006:
http://www.dfat.gov.au/geo/solomon_islands/solomon_islands_brief.html

Australian Federal Police, *A Brief History of the Australian Federal Police: 1979–2004*, Canberra, Australia: Australian Federal Police Museum, October 19, 2004a. As of September 15, 2006:
http://www.afp.gov.au/__data/assets/pdf_file/3728/historyaustralianfederalpolice.pdf

Australian Federal Police, *Annual Report, 2003–2004*, Canberra, Australia, November 26, 2004b. As of September 13, 2006:
http://www.afp.gov.au/__data/assets/pdf_file/3649/annual_report.pdf

Australian Government, Department of Defence, "24 December 2004: Rapid Response Capability on Operation Anode," *Regional Assistance to Solomon Islands, Operation Anode*, online image gallery, December 24, 2004. As of March 20, 2006:
http://www.defence.gov.au/opanode/images/gallery/241204/index.htm

———, "Operation Anode," Web page, last updated July 27, 2006. As of September 18, 2006:
http://www.defence.gov.au/opanode/

Australian House of Representatives, Official Hansard (transcript), 39th Parliament, First Session, Sixth Period, Canberra, Australia, June 6, 2000. As of September 18, 2006:
http://www.aph.gov.au/hansard/reps/dailys/dr060600.pdf

"Australian Reinforcements Land in Honiara," East-West Wire Service, April 19, 2006.

Batley, James, "The Role of RAMSI in Solomon Islands: Rebuilding the State, Supporting Peace," paper presented at Peace, Justice and Reconciliation Conference, Brisbane, Australia, March 31–April 3, 2005. As of January 31, 2006:
http://www.dfat.gov.au/media/speeches/department/050331_ramsi_paper_by_james_batley.html

Beckett, Ian F. W., and John Pimlott, eds., *Armed Forces and Modern Counter-Insurgency*, New York: St. Martin's Press, 1985.

Bennett, Major Vernon, New Zealand Army, interview with Russell W. Glenn, Wellington, New Zealand, November 21, 2005a.

———, email to Russell W. Glenn, Subject: Re: Duffer's, November 22, 2005b.

———, email to Russell W. Glenn, Subject: Re: RAND draft, March 23, 2006.

Bonser, Rear Admiral Mark, Royal Australian Navy, interview with Russell W. Glenn, Canberra, Australia, November 9, 2005.

Boulton, Lieutenant Colonel Donna, Australian Army, interview with Russell W. Glenn, Sydney, Australia, November 4, 2005.

Bowden, Rich, "'Children Overboard' Scandal Resurfaces," *Worldpress.org*, August 23, 2004. As of December 1, 2005:
http://www.worldpress.org/Asia/1918.cfm

Brandon, James, "To Fight Al Qaeda, US Troops in Africa Build Schools Instead," *Christian Science Monitor*, January 9, 2006. As of September 18, 2006:
http://www.csmonitor.com/2006/0109/p01s04-woaf.html

Breen, Bob, *Mission Accomplished: East Timor, The Australian Defence Force Participation in the International Forces East Timor (INTERFET)*, Crows Nest, Australia: Allen and Unwin, 2001.

British Army, Directorate General, Development and Doctrine, Army Doctrine Publication AC71819, *Land Operations*, UK Ministry of Defence, May 2005. As of September 13, 2006:
http://www.carlisle.army.mil/usacsl/divisions/pksoi/StaticDocuments/UK/050719_adp_land_ops_WEB-optimized.pdf

Bryant, Lieutenant Colonel James, Australian Army, "Analysis of Regional Assistance Mission to the Solomon Islands (RAMSI) 'Lessons Learnt,' Specifically Planning/Interagency Factors," draft provided to Russell W. Glenn, dated October 5, 2005a.

————, interview with Russell W. Glenn, Canberra, Australia, November 9, 2005b.

————, email to Russell W. Glenn, Subject: Re: SI, January 11, 2006.

Burns, Robert, "Deployments Stretching Army, Study Finds," Associated Press, January 25, 2006.

Byman, Daniel, "Going to War with the Allies You Have: Allies, Counterinsurgency, and the War on Terrorism," Carlisle, Pa.: Strategic Studies Institute, 2005. As of January 11, 2006:
http://www.strategicstudiesinstitute.army.mil/pdffiles /PUB630.pdf

Callwell, C. E., *Small Wars: Their Principles and Practice*, Wakefield, UK: EP Publishing Limited, [1906] 1976.

Central Intelligence Agency, map of Solomon Islands, January 1, 1989, in ReliefWeb, "Solomon Islands," undated Web page. Map, as of July 18, 2006:
http://www.reliefweb.int/rw/RWB.NSF/db900LargeMaps/SKAR-64GBHC?OpenDocument

————, *The World Factbook*, Washington, D.C., 2005. Updated (2006) edition, as of September 12, 2006:
https://www.cia.gov/cia/publications/factbook/index.html

————, "Solomon Islands," *The World Factbook,* Washington, D.C., 2006. As of July 18, 2006:
https://www.cia.gov/cia/publications/factbook/geos/bp.html

Clarke, Group Captain Shaun, Royal New Zealand Air Force, interview with Russell W. Glenn, Wellington, New Zealand, November 21, 2005.

Clausewitz, Carl von, *On War,* Michael Howard and Peter Peret, eds. and trans., Princeton, N.J.: Princeton University Press, 1976.

Clutterbuck, Richard L., *The Long Long War: Counterinsurgency in Malaya and Vietnam,* N.Y.: Praeger, 1966.

Cox, John, and Joanne Morrison, "Solomon Islands Provincial Governance Information Paper," report to AusAID, October–November 2004. As of September 17, 2006:
http://www.ausaid.gov.au/publications/pdf/sols_provincial_gov.pdf

Crawford, John, and Glyn Harper, *Operation East Timor,* Auckland, New Zealand: Reed Books, 2001.

Crawshaw, Marion, interview with Russell W. Glenn, Wellington, New Zealand, November 18, 2005.

————, email to Russell W. Glenn, Subject: Re: RAND draft, March 23, 2006a.

————, email to Russell W. Glenn, Subject: Re: Reply to thoughts on RAND draft, March 26, 2006b.

Delk, James, "MOUT: A Domestic Case Study—The 1992 Los Angeles Riots," in Russell W. Glenn and Randall Steeb, *The City's Many Faces: Proceedings of the RAND Arroyo–MCWL–J8 UWG Urban Operations Conference, April 13–14, 1999,* Santa Monica, Calif.: RAND Corporation, 2000, pp. 81–156. As of September 13, 2006:
http://www.rand.org/pubs/conf_proceedings/CF148/

Desia, Raj, and Harry Eckstein, "Insurgency: The Transformation of Peasant Rebellion," *World Politics,* Vol. 42, No. 4, July 1990, pp. 441–465.

Downer, Alexander, "Solomon Islands Parliament Supports Australia's Offer," media release, Minister for Foreign Affairs, Australia, July 11, 2003a. As of August 24, 2005:
http://www.foreignminister. gov.au/releases/2003/fa084_03.html

————, "Australia Welcomes Further NZ Deployment to Solomon Islands," media release, Minister for Foreign Affairs, Australia, August 25, 2003b. As of August 24, 2005:
http://www.foreignminister.gov.au/releases/2003/fa105_03.html

————, "Australian RAMSI Police Office Killed in Honiara," media release, Minister for Foreign Affairs, Australia, December 22, 2004. As of September 13, 2006:
http://foreignminister.gov.au/releases/2004/fa184_04.html

————, "RAMSI: Second Anniversary," media release, Minister for Foreign Affairs, Australia, July 22, 2005. As of January 31, 2006:
http://foreignminister.gov.au/releases/2005/fa094_05.html

Downer, Alexander, and Chris Ellison, "Solomon Islands: Harold Keke Found Guilty," joint news release, Minister for Foreign Affairs and Minister for Justice and Customs, Australia, March 18, 2005. As of September 13, 2006:
http://foreignminister.gov.au/releases/2005/joint_ellison_solomon_islands_180305.html

Echevarria, Antulio J. II, *Fourth-Generation War and Other Myths*, Carlisle, Pa.: Strategic Studies Institute, November 2005. As of September 18, 2006:
http://www.strategicstudiesinstitute.army.mil/pdffiles/PUB632.pdf

Etherington, Mark, *Revolt on the Tigris: The Al-Sadr Uprising and the Governing of Iraq*, Ithaca, N.Y.: Cornell University Press, 2005.

European Centre on Pacific Issues, "Conflict and Resolution: Solomon Islands Update," November 14, 2003. As of January 31, 2006:
http://www.antenna.nl/ecsiep/conflict/si/14-11-03.html

Evans, Major General Mark, Australian Army, interview with Russell W. Glenn, Brisbane, Australia, July 18, 2003.

Flowers, Lieutenant Colonel Quentin, Australian Army, interview (accompanied by written remarks) with Russell W. Glenn, Sydney, Australia, November 3, 2005.

"FLW Working Construct: Complex Warfighting Modes of Operation: Joint Land Manoeuvre and Control Operations," Australian Army briefing provided to Russell W. Glenn by Colonel D. Freeman, Australian Army, June 2005.

Foster, Lieutenant Colonel Luke, Australian Army, interview with Russell W. Glenn, Canberra, Australia, November 9, 2005.

Fraenkel, Jon, "The Coming Anarchy in Oceania? A Critique of the 'Africanisation' of the South Pacific Thesis," Suva, Fiji: University of the South Pacific, Department of Economics, Working Paper No. 2003/2, February 2003. As of September 13, 2006:
http://www.usp.ac.fj/fileadmin/files/schools/ssed/economics/working_papers/2003/wp2003_02.pdf

Freeman, Colonel Don, "Complex Warfighting Modes of Operation: Joint Land Manoeuvre and Control Operations," slide presentation, Joint Urban Warrior 2005, Potomac, Md., June 2005.

Frewen, Lieutenant Colonel John J., email to James Bryant, Subject: SEC: UNCLASSIFIED: Re: RAMSI STUFF, September 22, 2005a.

————, Australian Army, interview with Russell W. Glenn, Canberra, Australia, November 11, 2005b.

————, email to Dr. Russell W. Glenn, Subject: Re: Unclassified: RAND RAMSI draft, April 13, 2006.

Fry, Greg, "Political Legitimacy and the Post-colonial State in the Pacific: Reflections on Some Common Threads in the Fiji and Solomon Islands Coups," *Pacifica Review: Peace, Security, and Global Change*, Vol. 12, No. 3., October 2000, pp. 295–304.

Gray, Alfred M., "Irregular Warfare II Conference Report: 'Creating Stability in an Unstable World,'" Marine Corps Research Center, Quantico, Va., July 11–12, 2005.

Greener-Barcham, Beth, "Military and Police in Overseas Assistance Missions," in *Securing a Peaceful Pacific*, John Henderson and Greg Watson, eds., Christchurch, New Zealand: University of Canterbury Press, 2005.

Greer, James K., "Operation Knockout: COIN in Iraq," *Military Review*, November–December 2005, pp. 16–19. As of September 18, 2006: http://usacac.army.mil/CAC/milreview/download/English/NovDec05/greer.pdf

Headquarters, U.S. Department of the Army, Field Manual 100-5, *Operations*, Washington, D.C., August 1982.

————, Field Manual 100-5, *Operations*, Washington, D.C., May 1986.

————, Field Manual 3-0, *Operations*, Washington, D.C., June 2001. As of September 13, 2006: http://www.dtic.mil/doctrine/jel/service_pubs/fm3_0a.pdf

————, Field Manual 3-07.22, *Counterinsurgency Operations*, Washington, D.C., October 2004. As of September 23, 2006: http://www.fas.org/irp/doddir/army/fmi3-07-22.pdf

Headquarters, U.S. Department of the Army, and Headquarters, U.S. Air Force, Field Manual 100-20/Air Force Pamphlet 3-20, *Military Operations in Low Intensity Conflict*, Washington, D.C., December 5, 1990. As of December 8, 2005: http://www.globalsecurity.org/military/library/policy/army/fm/100-20/index.html

Headquarters, U.S. Department of the Army, and Headquarters, U.S. Marine Corps, Field Manual 3-24/Marine Corps Reference Publication 3-33.5, *Counterinsurgency* (initial draft), Washington, D.C.: Headquarters, U.S. Department of the Army, February 2006. Final draft (June 2006), As of September 13, 2006: http://www.fas.org/irp/doddir/army/fm3-24fd.pdf

Headquarters, U.S. Marine Corps, *Small Wars Manual*, Washington, D.C., 1987.

Heilbrunn, Otto, *Partisan Warfare*, London, UK: George Allen and Unwin, 1962.

Hegarty, David, "Peace Monitoring in the Solomon Islands," *Trust and Verify*, No. 99, September–October 2001, pp. 1–3. As of September 13, 2006:
http://www.vertic.org/assets/TV99.pdf

Hill, Robert, and Alexander Downer, "Australia Strengthens Military Presence in Solomon Islands," joint media release, Minister of Defence and Minister for Foreign Affairs, Australia, December 22, 2004. As of August 24, 2005:
http://www.foreignminister.gov.au/releases/2004/joint_solomon.html

History of Revolutionary Warfare, Volume 1: Introduction to the Study of the History of Revolutionary Warfare, West Point, N.Y.: U.S. Military Academy at West Point, Department of History, 1984.

Hoffman, Bruce, "Insurgency and Counterinsurgency in Iraq," Santa Monica, Calif.: RAND Corporation, OP-127-IPC/CMEPP, 2004. As of September 15, 2006:
http://www.rand.org/pubs/occasional_papers/OP127/

Hosmer, Stephen T., *The Army's Role in Counterinsurgency and Insurgency*, Santa Monica, Calif.: RAND Corporation, R-3947-A, 1990.

Houston, Bill, Senior Historian, Australian Army Headquarters, interview with Russell W. Glenn, Canberra, Australia, July 14, 2003.

Howard, The Hon. John, transcript of press conference, subject: "Solomon Islands, David Hicks, ABC, Tony Blair, Iraq, Newspoll, meeting with indigenous leaders," Canberra, July 22, 2003. As of January 30, 2006:
http://www.pm.gov.au/news/interviews/Interview382.html

Howard, Lieutenant Colonel John, New Zealand Army, "Multinational Force Integration in Regional Deployments," briefing presented at Urban Asia Pacific Conference, Surfers Paradise, Australia, November 17, 2005.

Hutcheson, Lieutenant Colonel John, Australian Army, "Wars of Conscience: Human Rights, National Security and Australia's Defence Policy," Canberra, Australia: Strategic and Defence Studies Centre, CP-140, 2001.

———, "Helping a Friend: An Australian Military Commander's Perspective on the Regional Assistance Mission to the Solomon Islands," *Australian Army Journal*, Vol. 2, No. 2, Autumn 2005a, pp. 47–55. As of September 16, 2006:
http://www.defence.gov.au/ARMY/LWSC/Publications/journal/AAJ_Autumn05/AAJ_Autumn05_hutcheson_7.pdf

———, interview with Russell W. Glenn, Canberra, Australia, November 8, 2005b.

———, email to Russell W. Glenn, Subject: UNCLAS COIN Paper, May 25, 2006.

"The In and Out Prime Minister," *Economist*, April 27, 2006, p. 48.

Joint Chiefs of Staff, Joint Publication 1-02, *Department of Defense Dictionary of Military and Associated Terms*, Washington, D.C., April 12, 2001, as amended through August 8, 2006. As of September 13, 2006:
http://www.dtic.mil/doctrine/jel/new_pubs/jp1_02.pdf

Kabutaulaka, Tarcisius Tara, "Howard Hears the Solomons Drumbeat," *Pacific Islands Report*, June 20, 2003. As of September 18, 2006:
http://archives.pireport.org/archive/2003/june/06-20-tara.htm

Kilcullen, David, "The Political Consequences of Military Operations in Indonesia: A Fieldwork Analysis of the Political Power-Diffusion Effects of Guerrilla Conflict," dissertation, School of Politics, University College, University of New South Wales, 2000.

———, "East Timor—Model of a Modern Deployment?" in *Battles Near and Far: A Century of Overseas Deployment*, Canberra, Australia: Army History Unit, 2005.

———, "Globalisation and the Development of Indonesian Counterinsurgency Tactics," *Small Wars and Insurgencies*, Vol. 17, No. 1, March 2006a, pp. 44–64.

———, email and attached notes sent to Russell W. Glenn, Subject: DRR3909_4_14b_06, May 18, 2006b.

Kitson, Frank, *Bunch of Five*, London, UK: Faber and Faber, 1977.

———, *Warfare as a Whole*, London, UK: Faber and Faber, 1987.

Lambert, Geoffrey C., "CSIS," briefing provided to Russell W. Glenn, November 2005.

Laqueur, Walter, *Guerrilla*, London, UK: Weidenfeld and Nicolson, 1977.

Lewis, Major General Duncan, Australian Army, interview with Russell W. Glenn, Sydney, Australia, July 15, 2003.

Londey, Peter, *Other People's Wars: A History of Australian Peacekeeping*, Crows Nest, Australia: Allen and Unwin, 2004.

Maher, Michael, "Islands in the Storm," *The Bulletin*, June 20, 2000.

"Malaita Eagles Force/Isatabu Freedom Movement," *GlobalSecruity.org*, last updated April 27, 2005. As of September 18, 2006:
http://www.globalsecurity.org/military/world/para/solomons.htm

Manton, Jeremy, Counselor, Embassy of Australia, Washington, D.C., briefing presented at Defence R&D Canada Valcartier Urban Operations Conference, Quebec City, Canada, December 1, 2004.

Manwaring, Max G., *Shadows of Things Past and Images of the Future: Lessons for the Insurgencies in our Midst*, Carlisle, Pa.: U.S. Army War College, November 2004. As of September 18, 2006:
http://www.strategicstudiesinstitute.army.mil/pdffiles/PUB587.pdf

Mao Tse-tung, "The Three Stages of the Protracted War," in *The Guerrilla Reader*, Walter Laqueur, ed., N.Y.: Meridian, 1977.

Matarazzo, David P., *Far More Intellectual Than a Bayonet Charge: The Need for Joint Unconventional Warfare Doctrine*, Fort Leavenworth, Kans.: U.S. Army Command and General Staff College, Academic Year 2003–2004. As of September 18, 2006:
http://www.smallwarsjournal.com/documents/matarazzo.pdf

McCuen, John J., "Fighting Wars Within the Population," transcript of presentation, undated.

———, *The Art of Counter-Revolutionary War: The Strategy of Counter-Insurgency*, Harrisburg, Pa.: Stackpole, 1966.

———, "The Threat of Terrorism," transcript of presentation, 2005.

McDevitt, Ben, interview with Russell W. Glenn, Canberra, Australia, November 8, 2005a.

———, untitled speech, undated, copy presented to Russell W. Glenn, Canberra, Australia, November 11, 2005b.

———, email to Russell W. Glenn, Subject: McDevitt, July 25, 2006.

McDonald, Colin, "Out of the Ashes—A New Criminal Justice System for East Timor," paper presented at the International Society of the Reform of Criminal Law 15th International Conference, Canberra, Australia, August 30, 2001. As of March 14, 2006:
http://www.isrcl.org/Papers/McDONALD.pdf

McFate, Montgomery, and Andrea V. Jackson, "The Objective Beyond War: Counterinsurgency and the Four Tools of Political Competition," *Military Review*, January–February 2006, pp. 13–26. As of September 18, 2006:
http://usacac.army.mil/CAC/milreview/English/JanFeb06/McFate3.pdf

McLaurin, R. D., and R. Miller, "Urban Counterinsurgency: Case Studies and Implications for U.S. Military Forces," Technical Memorandum 14-89, Aberdeen Proving Ground, Md.: U.S. Army Human Engineering Laboratory, October 1989.

McPhedran, Ian, "Huts On Way for Cops in a Swamp," *Herald Sun* (Melbourne, Australia), October 9, 2003, p. 30.

"Mission Helpem Fren: A Review of the Regional Assistance Mission to Solomon Islands," Report of the Pacific Island Forum Eminent Persons Group, May 2005. As of September 17, 2006:
http://pidp.eastwestcenter.org/pireport/special/Forum_RAMSI_review.pdf

Mockaitis, Thomas R., *British Counterinsurgency, 1919–60*, New York: St. Martin's Press, 1990.

Molnar, Andrew R., *Human Factors Considerations of Undergrounds in Insurgencies*, Washington, D.C.: Special Operations Research Office, 1965.

————, "Introduction to Insurgency," in *History of Revolutionary Warfare, Volume I: Introduction to the Study of History of Revolutionary Warfare*, West Point, N.Y.: United States Military Academy at West Point, Department of History, 1984.

Monterola, Major Simon, Australian Army, interview with Russell W. Glenn, Canberra, Australia, November 8, 2005.

Morrison, Scott A., "The Sheathed Sword," Council for Emerging National Security Affairs, 2003. As of September 18, 2006: http://www.censa.net/publications/Scott_Morrison/Morrison_Sept182003.pdf

Myers, John, "Heat Takes Toll on Sweaty Sappers," *Evening Standard* (Palmerston North, New Zealand), August 6, 2003, p. 3.

National Australia Day Council, "Australian of the Year Awards, 2005: Ben McDevitt AM APM," 2005. As of September 16, 2006: http://www.australianoftheyear.gov.au/pages/bio.asp?pID=119

New Zeland Army, "Army Overseas Operations: Solomon Islands," last updated July 31, 2006. As of September 18, 2006: http://www.army.mil.nz/army-overseas/operations/solomon+islands/default.htm

New Zealand Police, "Overseas Assistance: Solomon Islands," last updated August 2, 2006. As of September 15, 2006: http://www.police.govt.nz/service/overseas/solomonislands.html

New Zealand's International Aid and Development Agency, "Solomon Islands Fact Sheet," October 2004. As of January 13, 2006: http://www.nzaid.govt.nz/library/docs/factsheet-solomons.pdf

————, "Who Is NZAID?" last updated July 1, 2006. As of September 15, 2006: http://www.nzaid.govt.nz/about/index.html

Noble, Peter, interview with Russell W. Glenn, Wellington, New Zealand, November 19, 2005.

————, email to Russell W. Glenn, Subject: Re: RAND draft, March 27, 2006.

Office of the United Nations Resident Coordinator, United Nations Development Programme, "Common Country Assessment: Solomon Islands," final draft, Suva, Fiji, March 23, 2002.

Oxfam Community Aid Abroad, "Australian Intervention in the Solomons: Beyond Operation Helpem Fren–An Agenda for Development in the Solomon Islands," Fitzroy, Australia, August 2003a. As of September 18, 2006: http://www.oxfam.org.au/world/pacific/solomons/report.pdf

————, "Solomon Islands—Looking Beyond the Military Intervention to an Agenda for Development," August 25, 2003b. As of September 18, 2006: http://www.oxfam.org.au/media/article.php?id=110

"Peacekeeper Shot Dead in Solomons," *BBC News*, December 22, 2004. As of March 7, 2006:
http://news.bbc.co.uk/1/hi/world/asia-pacific/4116931.stm

Petraeus, David H., "Learning Counterinsurgency: Observations from Soldiers in Iraq," *Military Review*, January–February 2006, pp. 2–12.

Pike, Douglas, PAVN: People's Army of Vietnam, Novato, Calif.: Presidio, 1986.

Ponzio, Richard, "The Solomon Islands: The UN and Intervention by Coalitions of the Willing," *International Peacekeeping*, Vol. 12, No. 2, Summer 2005, pp. 173–188.

Pustay, John S., *Counterinsurgency Warfare*, N.Y.: Free Press, 1965.

Race, Jeffrey, *War Comes to Long An: Revolutionary Conflict in a Vietnamese Province*, Berkeley, Calif.: University of California Press, 1972.

Raffaele, Paul, "In John They Trust," *Smithsonian*, Vol. 36, February 2006, pp. 70–77.

"RAMSI Leaders Brief Pacific Neighbors," *Port Vila Presse* (Vanuatu), July 2, 2004. As of January 31, 2006:
http://www. news.vu/en/news/RegionalNews/ramsi-leaders-brief-pacif.shtml

"RAMSI Press Conference: RAMSI's Objectives for 2004," transcript of press conference led by Nick Warner, Ben McDevitt, Quentin Flowers, and Catherine Walker, Lelei Resort, Guadalcanal, February 16, 2004. As of September 13, 2006:
http://www.dfat.gov.au/media/transcripts/2004/040116_ramsi.html

Rathmell, Andrew, "Planning Post-Conflict Reconstruction in Iraq: What Can We Learn?" *International Affairs*, Vol. 81, No. 5, October 2005, pp. 1013–1038.

ReliefWeb, "Solomon Islands," undated Web page. As of September 12, 2006:
http://www.reliefweb.int/rw/dbc.nsf/doc104?OpenForm&rc=5&cc=slb

Rice, Edward E., *Wars of the Third Kind: Conflict in Underdeveloped Countries*, Berkeley, Calif.: University of California Press, 1988.

Rixon, Peter, "Solomon Islands: One Deployment Too Many?" Department of the Parliamentary Library, Canberra, Australia, Research Note No. 4, July 30, 2003. As of September 28, 2006:
http://www.aph.gov.au/LIBRARY/Pubs/rn/2003-04/04rn04.pdf

Ryan, Alan, "'Primary Responsibilities and Primary Risks': Australian Defence Force Participation in the International Force East Timor," Canberra Australia: Australian Land Warfare Studies Centre, Study Paper No. 304, November 2000. As of September 13, 2006:
http://www.defence.gov.au/army/lwsc/Publications/SP/SP%20304.pdf

Schiff, Zeev, and Raphael Rothstein, *Fedayeen: Guerrillas Against Israel*, N.Y.: David McKay, 1972.

Schnaubelt, Christopher M., "After the Fight: Interagency Operations," *Parameters: U.S. Army War College Quarterly*, Vol. 35, No. 4, Winter 2005–2006, pp. 47–61. As of September 17, 2006:
http://www.carlisle.army.mil/USAWC/Parameters/05winter/schnaube.pdf

Schwarz, Benjamin, American *Counterinsurgency Doctrine and El Salvador: The Frustrations of Reform and the Illusions of Nation Building*, Santa Monica, Calif.: RAND Corporation, R-4042-USDP, 1991.

Singh, Colonel Peter, Australian Army interview with Russell W. Glenn, Puckapunyal, Australia, July 16, 2003.

Smith, Rupert, *The Utility of Force: The Art of War in the Modern World*, London, UK: Allen Lane, 2005.

Strickland, Adam. "Reinventing the Counterinsurgency Wheel," *Small Wars Journal*, Vol. 2, July 2005, pp. 13–17. As of September 18, 2006:
http://www.smallwarsjournal.com/documents/swjvol2.pdf

Taber, Robert, *The War of the Flea: A Study of Guerrilla Warfare Theory and Practice*, London, UK: Paladin, 1969.

"The Testament of Solomons: RAMSI and International State-Building," Sydney, Australia: Lowy Institute for International Policy, March 2006.

Thomson, Lieutenant Colonel Bill, Australian Army, interview with Russell W. Glenn, Surfers Paradise, Australia, November 17, 2005.

Thompson, Loren B., *Low-intensity Conflict: The Pattern of Warfare in the Modern World*, Lexington, Mass.: Lexington Books, 1989.

Thompson, Robert, *Defeating Communist Insurgency: Experiences from Malaya and Vietnam*, London, UK: Chatto and Windus, 1970.

Trinquier, Roger, *Modern Warfare: A French View of Counterinsurgency*, Ft. Leavenworth, Kans.: U.S. Army Command and General Staff College, 1985. As of September 15, 2006:
http://www-cgsc.army.mil/carl/resources/csi/trinquier/trinquier.asp

Tunnah, Helen, "Top Cop Backs Canberra's Actions in Pacific," *New Zealand Herald*, August 17, 2005. As of September 18, 2006:
http://www.nzherald.co.nz/category/print.cfm?c_id=32&objectid=10341103

University of Texas Libraries, University of Texas at Austin, map of west Pacific islands, undated. As of September 12, 2006:
http://www.lib.utexas.edu/maps/australia/west_pacific_islands98.jpg

Wainwright, Elsina, *Our Failing Neighbour: Australia and the Future of Solomon Islands*, Canberra, Australia: Australian Strategic Policy Institute, June 2003. As of September 13, 2006:
http://www.aspi.org.au/uploaded/pubs/solomons.pdf

———, "How is RAMSI Faring? Progress, Challenges, and Lessons Learned," *Strategic Insights*, Australian Strategic Policy Institute, April 12, 2005. As of September 18, 2006:
http://www.aspi.org.au/uploaded/pubs/SI_solomons.pdf

Warner, Nick, "Message to the People of Solomon Islands," speech, July 24, 2003. As of January 31, 2006:
http://www.dfat.gov.au/media/speeches/department/240703_warner_soli.html

———, "Operation Helpem Fren: Rebuilding the Nation of Solomon Islands," speech to National Security Conference, March 23, 2004a. As of September 13, 2006:
http://www.dfat.gov.au/media/speeches/department/040323_nsc_ramsi.html

———, "Message to the People of Solomon Islands: RAMSI's One Year Anniversary," speech, July 24, 2004b. As of September 18, 2006:
http://www.dfat.gov.au/media/speeches/department/040724_ramsi_1_year_anniversary.html

———, interview with Russell W. Glenn, Canberra, Australia, November 11, 2005.

Watson, James, "A Model Pacific Solution? A Study of the Deployment of the Regional Assistance Mission to Solomon Islands," Canberra, Australia: Land Warfare Studies Centre, Working Paper No. 126, October 2005a. As of September 13, 2006:
http://www.defence.gov.au/army/lwsc/Publications/WP/WP_126.pdf

———, interview with Russell W. Glenn, Canberra, Australia, November 10, 2005b.

Weller, Major Charles, Australian Army, interview with Russell W. Glenn, Canberra, Australia, November 8, 2005.

Wing, Ian, "Applying First Principles: A National Crisis Management Approach for Australia," undated briefing.

Yates, Lawrence A., *Powerpack: U.S. Intervention in the Dominican Republic, 1965–1966*, Leavenworth Papers, No. 15, Fort Leavenworth, Kans.: Combat Studies Institute, U.S. Army Command and General Staff College, 1988. As of September 18, 2006:
http://www-cgsc.army.mil/carl/resources/csi/yates/yates.asp

Zinn, Christopher, "Australian Troops to Quell Solomon Islands Unrest," transcript, *The 7.30 Report*, Australian Broadcasting Corporation, April 19, 2006. As of September 15, 2006:
http://www.abc.net.au/7.30/content/2006/s1619470.htm